I0002925

Virtualization and IT Project Success

By

Richard Scroggins

MS, Capella University, 2012

BS, Capella University, 2011

AA, Blinn College, 1996

Doctoral Study Submitted in Partial Fulfillment

of the Requirements for the Degree of

Doctor of Applied Science

Concordia College

May 2017

Dedication:
To Samantha, for all that you are; to Archer, for all that you will be.

"I have steadily endeavored to keep my mind free so to give up any hypothesis, however much beloved, as soon as facts are shown to be opposed to it."

—Charles Darwin

Sections:

Chapter 1: Virtualization

The History, Current Usage, and Future of Virtualization

Trends in virtualization are always changing. As the technology matures and advances are made, there are more options open to administrators and more cost saving virtualization projects that can be implemented. The website "Virtualize Your IT Infrastructure" by the VMWare Company gives you some idea of the capability using the VMWare product, which is simply one of several virtualization options. When compared with other hypervisors like Hyper V, or KVM, the features of VMWare's ESX and ESXi stand out. (Virtualize Your IT Infrastructure, 2012). A complete overview of the VMWare products and how they are applicable to each stage in the virtualization process is given, and also the various options or platforms for virtualization with each product. Connor (2004) makes the point that server virtualization is moving from small markets to the mainstream and that the rate of implementation is steadily increasing. The article also addresses the race to keep up with processor technology by VMWare and others (Connor, 2004). As evidence for this, Connor (2004) says, “If you look at processor trends, both Intel and AMD have shifted from increasing the clock speed of their processors to, increasing the number of processor cores on a single chip," says Michael Mullaney, vice president of marketing for VMware.

"Going forward, you are going to find out that even a two-CPU server actually has four processors" (p. 01) Connor (2004) says "Virtualization is moving from a niche market into the mainstream, especially since Microsoft entered the market" (p. 01) This makes it clear that this is a project topic that is worth pursuing. This is a technology that is just now permeating into the main stream and the future of the technology is leading in a direction of more and more implementation.

Spiegel (2006) makes the case that there is business benefits in application and server virtualization, “Application virtualization is the new fancy trendy name for server-based computing. However, instead of installing applications on desktops, the applications are installed in a server farm for secure, remote access. Server virtualization allows you to take multiple physical servers and create the same number of virtual servers, or "machines," on one host physical server” (p. 01). By simplifying the structure and management, the business gets a benefit, or multiple benefits. This also supports the assertion that there is a business benefit to application and server virtualization. This assertion is further supported by the point that centralizing servers and application onto hypervisors, or rather servers running a virtual server product, like VMWare’s ESXi, can give the business several things that add value and support the ROI. Those things being; reduced maintenance costs, reduced hardware costs, reduced licensing cost, reduced administration costs, and increased disaster recovery security.

Hassell (2007) gives us a summary of his article in the abstract section when he says, "Virtualization, the move from real, physical hardware to virtual hardware is being seen as one of the "next big things" in IT. There are more virtualization options for IT departments than ever before, including XenSource Inc's and Virtual Iron Software Inc's open-source applications, Microsoft Corp's Virtual Server and VMware Inc's venerable products. But if you are new to this party, you might not know how to get started." (p. 01). Hassell (2007) gives a broad overview of the topic and a launching point to explore the topic of virtualization and some of the options that are available, phases of implementation. (Hassell, 2007). Hassell (2007) is experienced in this field and is therefore a valued source for this subject matter. Hassell (2007) breaks down the process step by step, "The first step in virtualization is determining if you have the right type of infrastructure to support it. Look for a lot of machines doing similar tasks, and make sure you have more than 10 of them. For 10 or fewer, the payoff is questionable." (p. 01).

Virtualization and IT Project Success

Reducing redundant hardware through virtualization as a strategy is the key point made by McAllister (2007). McAllister (2007) states, “In today's complex IT environments, server virtualization simply makes sense. Redundant server hardware can rapidly fill enterprise datacenters to capacity; each new purchase drives up power and cooling costs even as it saps the bottom line. With virtualization, you can dynamically fire up and take down virtual servers, each of which basically fools an operating system into thinking the virtual machine is actual hardware. The most popular method of virtualization uses software called a hypervisor to create a layer of abstraction between virtual servers and the underlying hardware.” (p. 01). This is a valid statement, and the core idea of the process behind virtualization. This article also compares the state of virtualization now with the past and names the major players in the environment like VMWare and Microsoft (McAllister, 2007). McAllister (2007) validates not only one of my suggested methods of business benefit, which is cost savings, but it also provides context for the history and installation options of a virtual environment. McAllister (2007) also details many options that are available to administrators. One main point that is important to present is the time saving and options that are available to server administrators.

Bele and Desai (2012) look at virtualization from a slightly broader perspective. Beyond the hypervisor platform alone, Bele and Desai (2012) look at how virtual host tie into the rest of your environment, like SAN with a look at storage virtualization. Bele and Desai (2012) detail how all of these components are related, "Server Virtualization plays key role to resolve such problems. It abstracts the resources from the applications that utilize them and can be applied to many platforms. Virtualization Technology has been adopted at large level by many data centers in the industry. It provides benefits like server consolidation, live migration, data security, less power consumption etc. Same time Storage Virtualization abstracts physical storage (SAN, NAS) resources from front end applications running in the system. Storage virtualization is useful to maintain large volume of data with continuous backup facility" (p.01). Bele and Desai (2012) look at the idea or concept of virtualization beyond mere server virtualization and gives us other lines to explore when looking at the value of virtualization on the whole. Any technology that really permeates the market typically is able to perform multiple functions, but is usually part of a larger technology.

Schultz (2009) looks at the beginnings, present, and future of virtualization. Schultz (2009) gives this insight, "With information virtualization, an enterprise is able to assemble a single view, or profile, of a client by bringing together information stored in multiple repositories. Virtualizing the workspace is the next logical step, Bishop says. While leading edge enterprises are striving toward this virtual nirvana, the majority of companies are baby-stepping their way through current-generation virtualization projects. What's next for them is more about growing the virtual server environment, integrating virtualization across servers, storage and the network, extending virtualization to the desktop" (p. 01). Schultz (2009) shows some of the changes in virtualization technology in the past and is key to my report by helping to detail and shape the "where did we come from" perspective. However, Schultz (2009) also gives a sense of where we are going with the technology, specifically the subject of desktop virtualization.

Norall (2007) gives this insight on the potential and advantages of storage virtualization, "In addition to creating storage pools composed of physical disks from different arrays, storage virtualization provides a wide range of services, delivered in a consistent way. These stretch from basic volume management, including LUN masking, concatenation, and volume grouping and striping, to data protection and disaster recovery functionality, including snapshots and mirroring. In short, virtualization solutions can be used as a central control point for enforcing storage management policies and achieving higher SLAs." (p. 01). As with other aspects of virtualization, Norall (2007) makes the point that there are clear advantages to virtualizing your storage. Norall (2007) shows that virtualization as a technology encompasses more than just server virtualization, which is the most common modern use of the overall technology. However, Norall (2007) shows that there are many aspects of virtualization and that it can be applied to many different technologies within the computer science spectrum.

Peggy (2007) makes the connection between virtualization and cost savings as follows: "There are three key areas of potential benefits: space, time and money. Fewer systems deployed results in lower capital costs. If companies can put 10 applications on 10 machines onto one or two machines, not only is that less money spent on computers, but the amount of money spent on electricity to power and cool these boxes goes down, freeing up precious data center space as well." (p. 01). Peggy (2007) discusses lowering costs through virtualization, which is one of the main advantages of virtualization.

Kontzer (2010) details a history and projected future for the technology, "More than a decade after VMware introduced the first software that enabled x86 virtualization, the question facing most IT executives is no longer whether they plan to virtualize, but how far they plan to go...The long-term potential of virtualization speaks to an issue that transcends server spread, budget concerns and any other barriers that might get in the way of a virtualization investment: The exponential growth of data is causing IT environments to burst at the seams." (p. 01). Kontzer (2010) explores not only the origin of the adoption of virtualization, but also the growth of virtualization in the industry, and what factors influence a company to make the investment in virtualization technology.

Kovar (2008) reveals the research that shows the current growth pattern of the virtualization technology. Kovar (2008) writes, "Solution providers are turning server virtualization, one of the fastest-growing segments of the IT market, into their very own gravy train. According to two recent exclusive CMP Channel surveys, solution providers said server virtualization is becoming a larger part of their business and it's also quickly becoming the catalyst for a wide range of other service offerings, including disaster recovery and data center consolidation." (p. 01). Everyone is talking about virtualization and just how hot it is, but can that growth or interest be measured? Yes, and Kovar (2008) shows that measurement and quantifies the growth factor.

Yoshida (2008) make the following revelation about storage virtualization," The initial approach to storage virtualization was to address virtualization in the storage-area network (SAN) because the SAN sat between the storage and servers and would cause the least disruption to these systems. However, after nearly a decade, this approach has not taken off while server virtualization has become widely accepted. The breakthrough came with the ability to virtualize physical logical unit numbers (LUNs) without the need to remap them by using a virtualization technique based on storage control units. This approach to storage virtualization is simple to implement. Storage virtualization will deliver significant efficiencies, cost savings, power and cooling benefits, as well as greater agility in aligning storage infrastructure to business requirements." (p. 01). One of the aspects of Yoshida's (2008) insight is to show that virtualization as a technology extends well beyond simple server virtualization.

Dubie (2009) goes deep into the concept and value of desktop virtualization, "Successful server virtualization deployments lead many IT managers to believe desktop virtualization would provide the same benefits. While that is partly true, companies need to be aware of how the two technologies differ" (p. 01). Dubie (2009) rightly points out that desktop virtualization is a technology not to be thought out lightly. Many industry experts focus on server virtualization, but Dubie (2009) suggests that desktop virtualization is the next big movement for virtualization. Dubie (2009) delves deep into the concept of desktop virtualization and reveals it to be a valid path for the mainstream IT department to pursue, but with caution and understanding.

Kennedy (2007) offers real solutions to the issue of desktop deployment, "Despite rumors to the contrary, virtualization is not just for the datacenter. From the most complex workstation applications to the simplest DLLs, virtualization is leaving an indelible mark on client computing. The idea behind application virtualization is to eliminate many of the support-draining configuration problems that plague conventional desktop implementations." (p.01) Kennedy (2007) takes on desktop virtualization from a slightly different perspective. Kennedy (2007) makes the point that desktop virtualization will continue to grow in the future. Hsieh (2008) lays out a strategy that is key to any virtualization project, as follows, "Virtualization has become one of the hottest information technologies in the past few years. Yet, despite the proclaimed cost savings and efficiency improvement, implementation of the virtualization involves high degree of uncertainty, and consequently a great possibility of failures. Experience from managing the VMware based project activities at several companies are reported as the examples to illustrate how to increase the chance of successfully implementing a virtualization project" (p.01). After all of the research, you need to be able to put it all together. Hsieh (2008) covers just that, a way to put it all together and implement a successful virtualization project.

Risk Management through Virtualization

Redundancy is very important in any environment as well as disaster recovery. Virtualization addresses these two risks very well. Virtual environments are highly redundant because the virtual images can be moved between different physical servers. This also makes the technology well suited as a disaster recovery solution. With physical servers, the data must be moved to a separate device like a tape or hard drive as individual files on the server. If it becomes necessary to restore a lost server, you first have to acquire a physical server, load the operating system, update it, and then start restoring files. With virtual servers, although you can still maintain the backup of individual files for ad hoc file restore, you can make an image of the entire server in real time, including even the information that is in the server's memory. As for the risks involved in migration, they are low. If you backup your physical server, and then perform a physical to virtual conversion, you can power down the physical server, but retain it and the data in the case that something goes wrong in the P2V conversion process. Risk management is a major part of the overall enterprise strategy. Risk management is a primary reason for the implementation of the virtual environment in the first place, above and beyond the many other benefits of virtualization. Almost anything that goes wrong in IT on any scale or within any scenario can be overcome if you have a good backup of your systems. Insistence on backups that are performed regularly, tested, and stored off site, whether this is on magnetic media or a remote SAN system, is important. The assurance that this is done will be part of the role of the CIO or IT Manager and should be an expectation from others in management that this service is being provided and documentation should also be provided as verification.

Violino (2009) not only emphasizes the importance of virtualization and disaster recovery as independent concepts, but also establishes a link between them. Violino (2009) says "Hordes of organizations have embraced server virtualization as they look to consolidate servers, reduce energy consumption in the data center, increase business agility and reduce costs. But there's life for virtualization beyond the server: The future of this technology likely will focus on client devices, and there's also great potential in areas such as business continuity, disaster recovery and capacity planning." (p. 01). Violino (2009) continues to establish the linkage and shared benefit, "Another likely trend is the use of virtualization for business continuity and disaster recovery. Efforts to provide adequate backup in the event of systems disruptions have become a high priority for many organizations, and some believe that virtualization is a natural fit for business continuity and disaster recovery" (p. 01).

Implementation of Virtualization using ESXi

Project Component: Stakeholders

Meeting with stakeholders is a very important step in any project. In fact, without knowing the needs of your stakeholders, it is impossible to successfully complete any project. In the case of this project, we need to meet with our stakeholders and determine several things: First, we need to verify the budget of the project. We need to know how much money is available for the project. This will let us know how may physical hosts that we can virtualize during the project and what type and quality of equipment and servers that we can purchase. Secondly, we need to verify the cutover window, which is the available time frame to make the move from the physical servers to the virtual servers using the P2V process. Lastly, we need to define the project scope. If we do not define the project well, the stakeholders may try to add tasks during the project, jeopardizing the completion. We have to try to eliminate any scope creep.

Project Component: Project Planning

Creating a project plan and timeline is important. We have to know how long the project is going to last, who is involved, and what the steps are that are involved in completion. Planning involves taking the needs of the stakeholders and the available budget, and designing a series of tasks with a timeline to do the most that we can within the available time and budget.

Steps to project completion:

1) Meet with the stakeholders

2) Create a project plan and timeline.

3) Purchase the physical hardware for the virtual environment.

4) Install ESXi on the physical hardware.

5) Use the P2V process on all physical servers. This may span several downtime windows.

6) Verify functionality with the stakeholders.

Project Component: Purchasing

Purchasing the physical hardware for the virtual environment is a key component of the project. Using the budget that we have acquired from our stakeholders and management, we must acquire the hardware that fits best with our needs and the money that we have available. This is why it is a good practice to get quotes from multiple hardware vendors, unless you have a set discount in place from a vendor like Dell or CDW. We also need to understand that the quoting process takes time, potentially several days depending on the scenario. Once we have and acceptable quote, we can purchase the hardware. Remember that once the order is placed for the hardware, it might take one or two weeks to arrive, so it is a good practice to have that time accounted for in your project plan.

Project Component: Installation

Installing ESXi on the physical hardware is a simple process, but there are several key things to remember. Once you have received the hardware, it must be unboxed, and then mounted in whatever racking system that you have in place. For most, that will be a standard four post rack or cabinet. Then, all of the power and network cabling, along with any KVM cables must be connected and secured. Once this is done, the ESXi software can be installed. By now, we should have downloaded the install disk from the web and burned a bootable DVD. Now we can turn on the first server with the bootable DVD in the drive and go through the simple installation process. The key information to have during the install process is a hostname for each physical server, and IP address, subnet mask, default gateway, and DNS information. I would not suggest the use of DHCP where servers are concerned. Also, we will need to set and remember a password for the root user during the installation. Once the ESXi operating system is installed on the server or servers, we then need to download and install the VMWare client onto a workstation so that we can manage the virtual servers.

Project Component: P2V Process

During the planning phase, we should have met with our stakeholders and determined our available windows of downtime for the physical to virtual conversions for all of the servers. This is a critical step in the project. If you have balanced out the load and space of each host server, you should be able to perform your physical to virtual conversions in a single weekend. However, you may need to schedule a follow up weekend just in case. The process of physical to virtual conversions usually takes one or two hours per server. The first step in this process is to download the VMWare converter tool and install it on all of the servers that are to be converted. One at a time, hopefully according to a set order, you can run the software to perform the conversion. During this process, it will be necessary to connect to the virtual host, so you will need the IP address along with the username and password to perform the conversion. Once the conversion is underway, there will be a one or two our wait, during this time, you can be running the process on servers that are being virtualized to different hosts. Once the process is complete, you will need to shut down the server that you just converted and start up the new virtual server using the desktop client. Once you assign the correct IP address information to the new virtual server, it should be ready for use.

Project Component: Verification

Verify functionality with the stakeholders or at least a test group is critical to the success of the project. Not only do we need to test that all applications work, but also that we have the performance that we expected. There may be a need to tweak the memory or other resources given to each virtual server so that you get the performance that you need.

Emerging Virtualization Technology

Virtualization technologies represent a very broad category of tools and technology that present many advantages to an organization. Virtualization is the concept or process of separating the logical from the physical. Rouse and Madden (2013), define server and desktop virtualization as "the concept of isolating a logical operating system instance from the client that is used to access it." (p. 1) Virtualization technologies allow an organization to literally do more with less as more technologies can be deployed onto a smaller set of physical hardware. For example, a virtualization software platform or hypervisor, can host virtual computers, servers, or devices that all exist on the same hardware and share physical resources but run different operating systems and existing within different virtual networks.

Much of the focus on virtualization technology in the industry and in the literature is on server virtualization. Despite this, server virtualization is neither the origin of virtualization nor the area where most innovation is emerging. The concept of virtualization in computer technology originated in the 1960's. Both IBM and MIT started working on virtualization technologies in the 1960's. The initial reference to virtual machine technology is from a discourse by MIT's Melinda Varían in the

1960's which introduced the compatible Time-Sharing System, or CTSS. (Ameen and Hamo, 2013) As stated, virtualization refers to a class of technologies rather than to one specific technology. The list below shows the major classifications of virtualization technology:

1) Mobile Virtualization
2) Data Virtualization
3) Memory Virtualization
4) Desktop Virtualization
5) Storage Virtualization
6) Network Virtualization
7) Application Virtualization
8) Grid Computing
9) Clustering
10) Server Virtualization

Ameen and Hamo, 2013

As stated, there is a focus in the industry on hardware or platform virtualization. This refers to creating a virtual machine, and is integral to the processes of server or desktop virtualization. This is the area of the technology where most administrator work with virtualization through hypervisor applications like VMWare or Microsoft's Hyper-V. This type of virtualization is popular, not only because of cost savings, but because it allows a server or computer running one operating system to also run a second operating system through virtualization. A common example of this would be a Microsoft windows pc running Windows 10 to use the virtual application to install and run Linux. It is also very common to install a Linux based hypervisor like VMWare's ESX on a server and then install Microsoft Windows Servers implementations on the same hardware.

Mobile Virtualization

Mobile virtualization is a true representation of an emerging area of virtualization technology. Mobile virtualization technology is an embedded software technology for use in mobile phones. In Mobile virtualization, the hardware and the data and applications are separated through the use of a hypervisor. This separation allows the phone to run in an optimized way and consume less power and memory. This design is incorporated across multiple phone, notebook, and tablet platforms, including Windows CE 5.0 and 6.0, Linux 2.6.x, Symbian 9.x, eCos, pITRON NORTi and pC/OS-II. (Ameen and Hamo, 2013) The primary driver for Mobile virtualization cost reduction in the manufacture of mobile phones. Mobile virtualization is tied directly to creating lower cost phones and is part of the business strategy for Android. A good example of this is Android's decision to produce smartphones without a separate baseband processor. This is achieved by running the baseband processor code and the applications in separate virtual machines on one processor. (Hookway, 2010)

Every industry has a need to reduce costs, and the mobile phone industry is no exception. Virtualization technologies reduce costs whether on the small scale like with phones or on the larger scale of servers and data centers. The cost savings of virtualization technology is what draws many stakeholders to investigate virtualization in the first place. Pogarcic, Krnjak, and Ozanic (2012) write, "The calculation proved that the application of virtualization software can lead to significant positive economic effects. In the observed example, a saving of almost 57.63% has been achieved." (p. 6). In the end, the technologies that organizations implement have to align with the financial needs of the organization, which usually means saving money. Few organizations can evaluate new technologies and exclude the financial impact, whether it is positive or negative. Our goal in IT should be to align our technology goals with the business.

Data Virtualization

Data virtualization is an emerging virtualization technology area that may be fruitful for new research, or for expanding existing research into. The research and discussion of virtualization technology is expanded into the overarching business intelligence models which includes software applications and analytical technologies that relate to the organizations data. Data virtualization, as a technology, abstracts data such that the source of individual aspects of the data whether databases, fields, etc. are presented on a common data access layer and the end client is blind to the source. This allows a single methodology for data access regardless of how or where the data is stored. (Ameen and Hamo, 2013) on the benefits of data virtualization technology, Bologa and Bologa (2011) write, " Providing a unified enterprise-wide data platform that feeds into consumer applications and meets the integration, analysis and reporting users' requirements is a wish that often involves significant time and resource consumption. As an alternative to developing a data warehouse for physical integration of enterprise data, the article presents data virtualization technology." (p. 110).

Another way to describe or think about data virtualization is that data virtualization is an approach to data management. As an approach to data management, data virtualization allows an application to retrieve and manipulate data without having any technical details about the data, including the format or physical location. This is very important for data integration or when data is presented from multiple sources. In stark contrast to the old methods of extracting, transferring, and importing data, data virtualization allows data access with no requirement for the data to move anywhere. In addition to saving costs, this reduces the risks associated with moving the data, like data corruption. Data virtualization does not impose any format on the data, so the reformatting is not needed, and can speed up implementations that access the data.

Memory Virtualization

Memory virtualization is an important aspect of modern computing, whether applied to an individual computing device, or a clustered environment. Memory virtualization technologies include expanding usable memory by using disk space, sharing memory between clustered devices, or sharing physical memory in a hypervisor environment. As an example, a guest operating system in a hypervisor environment expects to get a zero based memory environment, because it expects real hardware. The hypervisor, for instance VMWare's ESX, provides the illusion of physical hardware by adding an additional layer of memory addressing. (Ameen and Hamo, 2013) Memory virtualization also allows for the decoupling of physical hardware so that is can be shared in clustered or pooled environments. In this scenario, RAM, or Random Access Memory, is allocated by the virtualization software and shared out to a pool. Once this is done, then the memory in the pool is available to any computer in the cluster.

The memory virtualization application that many administrators are most familiar with is Microsoft Windows' virtual memory feature. As with other operating systems, the virtual memory feature in Windows is facilitated by managing memory using both hardware and software. In the case of Windows, memory addresses are mapped to virtual address rather than physical addresses. Then the system can direct these virtual addresses to either physical memory or to disk storage. This allows for optimized operation when running multiple programs, as the data in memory can be moved to disk when programs are idle. Compatible CPU hardware is also capable of mapping virtual addresses directly through the use of an embedded MMU, or Memory Management Unit. There are several benefits of using virtual memory in this way including freeing application from the requirement to use a shared memory space, more security from memory isolation, and being able to use more memory than is physically present in the computer system, a technique called paging.

Desktop/Application Virtualization

Desktop virtualization describes the ability to display a graphical desktop from one computer system on another computer system or smart display device. (Von Hagen, 2008) The simplest example of this is what people know as remote desktop. Desktop virtualization separates the desktop and application from the physical hardware. In this case the entire desktop can be virtualized or merely a single application, what is sometimes called application virtualization. Remote desktop in practice is a client/server configuration. Remote desktop is often used for remote support, high latency environments, or where secure or display only environments are desired. Remote desktop also allows the use of Microsoft Windows functionality on non-Windows devices like phones or tablets. Remote desktop can also be used as a cost saving measure by using inexpensive, low powered desktops that access virtual desktops on shared servers. This creates an environment that is centralized and easier to manage for administrators. The equivalent Linux application to Remote Desktop is X Windows. (Ameen and Hamo, 2013)

Desktop virtualization has many applications and benefits far beyond that of Remote Desktop alone. Gareiss (2008) writes, "An emerging technology destined to resolve many IT headaches without prescription medication is desktop virtualization. The technology helps IT staffs deliver functionality to remote workers faster and with more control than using traditional means. Desktop virtualization abstracts a desktop workload (operating system and applications) from desktop hardware." (p. 1). These features are facilitated by using a thin client on the client side. A thin client can be very simple in design, or offer all of the standard features of a desktop like sound and USB connection. While dedicated thin clients are available, some organizations use old desktops or inexpensive desktops in place of dedicated thin clients.

Storage Virtualization

According to Ameen and Hamo (2013), Storage Virtualization is "the emerging technology that creates logical abstractions of physical storage systems. Storage Virtualization has tremendous potential for simplifying storage administration and reducing costs for managing diverse storage assets." (p. 65). A simple example of storage virtualization is a storage array, or disk array. A storage array uses virtualization, along with hardware and software to enable better functionality and provide additional features. This includes increased speed and reliability. Storage arrays, which are specially designed computers, implement virtualization in one of two ways, block virtualization or file virtualization. Block virtualization is the separation of logical storage from physical storage; this separation allows for greater flexibility in managing and allocation the storage. File virtualization eliminates the dependency the data access request and the physical location of the data.

Storage virtualization gives flexibility to administrators, reduces costs by sharing resources, and adds speed and security to data functions. Weil (2007) writes, "At its most basic, storage virtualization makes scores of separate hard drives look to be one big storage pool. IT staffers spend less time managing storage devices, since some chores can be centralized. Backup and mirroring are also much faster because only changed data needs to be copied; this eliminates the need for scheduled storage management downtime." (p. 20). In the reccurring theme of the other virtualization technologies address, storage virtualization is primarily a cost saving measure, despite the other benefits. All of the benefits like reduced administration time and flexibility in the end result in lower cost for the organization, which helps to align IT with the financial goals of the organization. Storage virtualization requires complicated coordination of software and hardware configuration along with planning by implementers.

Network Virtualization

Network virtualization separates the network hardware from services that are delivered over the network. This is achieved by using both hardware and software together in a single administrative combination. This combination allows the separation of a network into virtual networks, called VLANs. This separation is very common in modern network environment and done for many reasons. On reason to use virtual networks is to separate users for security reasons. Another might be to simplify administration by providing different services on different virtual networks. A real world example of this practice is using virtual networking to separate voice and data traffic on a local network. In this scenario, the windows server and IP phone server both have DHCP addressing enabled, such that any device plugged into the network can receive an IP address from either server. However, you only want the windows server to give addresses to windows machine, and you only want the phones to get IP addresses from the phone server. Virtual networking allows an administrator to separate one network into two, so that the windows data is on one virtual network and the phone traffic is on another virtual network.

Again, network virtualization comes down to cost savings and economics. Teeter (2011) writes, "Healthcare organizations must test their network infrastructures for disaster recovery and emergency mode operations, yet most can't afford to operate the complicated protocols needed for safe testing. The Rapid Adjustable Network architecture offers a solution." (p. 48). According to Teeter (2011), virtual networks also add high availability, security, and flexibility to networks. While flexibility is nice, availability and security are critical needs for any network. Even in environments that are not in the business of life or death data, like healthcare, availability and security are a must for the organization. Most modern organizations grind to a halt when the network goes down because most of the work is on the network. Organizational process, documents, and systems all need the network to function and transmit data.

Grid Computing

Grid computing is another way to abstract or separate multiple computers or servers from the application or services that they are providing. Unlike a cluster however, in grid computing, the server do not need to be identical or even located together. Computing grids provide more capability, but require more coordination. (Ameen and Hamo, 2013) Grid computing can be thought of as a collection of computer resources from multiple locations that are working together to create a common goal. These resources may not be permanent and computing devices might only be part of the grid for a short time. A good example of this idea is the SETI at home program produced and distributed by SETI, or the Search for Extra Terrestrial Intelligence program. SETI designed and distributed software that connected user's desktops to SETI servers. This software ran on the desktop as a screen saver and processed data for SETI remotely when the computer would have otherwise been idle. The desktop software was provided for free and the installation was voluntary. At the time, Reichhardt (1999) wrote, "Three months after it began, Seti@home, an innovative scheme to enlist public help in the search for extraterrestrial intelligence (SETI), already has more than a million volunteers linking their PCs to the cause." (p.). Many other organizations have adopted this model, like the Human Genome Project. Grid computing clusters are sometime called super virtual computers.

The most important thing to understand about grid computing is that computers are brought together to achieve a common task, and which point the grid is dissolved. This grid typically using existing networks, much of which are public and often unsecured. Grid devices may enter or leave the grid suddenly, so contingencies must be programmed in to account for any unprocessed data. Computing grids are best suited for data that can be broken up and processed in different amounts, according to the ability of each device on the grid.

Clustering

Clustering is "a form of virtualization that makes several locally-attached physical systems appear to the application and end users as a single processing resource. This differs significantly from other virtualization technologies, which normally do the opposite, i.e. making a single physical system appear as multiple independent operating environments." (Ameen and Hamo, 2013, p. 65) Unlike a computing grid, clusters are built to be permanent, at least for the life of the application, which may mean years or decades. The hardware in clustered environments must have physical interconnectivity and the server hardware must be nearly identical. In a clustered environment, one system does the processing or work and the other system or systems are idle, at least in terms of that function. Only when needed, like in a disaster, does another computer take over control of that process. In a cluster, the individual computers are called nodes. In the typical design, each node in the clusters will be the primary node for one function. Cluster nodes are also connected to the same storage device, usually a storage array.

A simple example of a cluster might be two servers running Microsoft Windows Cluster Services. In the scenario, there is a file share and several printers being shared. On each server, the file share and the printers would be configured identically. Each server would have access to the cluster configuration utility where the file share service and printer share service could be monitored and changed. In an active-active configuration, one server would handle the file share and have the service assigned to it by the cluster management tool. The other server would have the printer service assigned to it. This configuration makes use of the computing power of each server to do something rather than sit idle. If there is a failure, one service would fail over to the server that was still up and functioning. In an active-passive configuration, one server would run both the file share and printer share services and the other server would stay idle until needed.

Server Virtualization

This paper has thus far included research and commentary on many forms of virtualization technology. However, server virtualization, in common parlance is the "big enchilada." Server virtualization technologies drive the industry and provide the computing backbones for organizations. Cloud computing, remote hosting, and virtual private servers all rely on server virtualization technology. HP (2009) defines server virtualization as referring to "abstracting, or masking, a physical server resource to make it appear different logically to what it is physically. In addition, server virtualization includes the ability for an administrator to relocate and adjust the machine workload." In other words server virtualization takes the resources of one computer or server and divides them up among guest operating systems that are unaware, for lack of a better term, of the host hardware or even that they themselves are virtual. This is facilitated by a type of software called a hypervisor. There are many hypervisors available, but one that has a very large footprint is VMWare's ESX platform. Hypervisors are able to facilitate not only the running of multiple virtualized systems, but also systems that vary in their operating system. Hypervisors are even able to host systems that would not be able to run on the host hardware through a process called emulation.

There are many advantages of server virtualization including cost savings, flexibility, performance advantages, and the optimization of resources. Server virtualization is a streamlining and optimizing technology that can have a significant impact on an organization. Bridges (2013) writes, "Visualization is an enabling technology that allows multiple operating system environments to be consolidated onto a single server, which reduces the amount of hardware that is required to run the entire bank's infrastructure. Adding virtualization technologies changes the shape of the existing IT infrastructure. A bank can also choose to outsource some IT workloads to cloud providers. In that case, it is the cloud service providers that use virtualization technologies to enhance their ability to manage their hosting infrastructures." (p. 14).

Summary

As shown, there are many different types of virtualization technology, each with unique benefits and risks. One thing that these virtualization categories have in common, however, is that they are changing as new virtualization technologies emerge, and the label of virtualization is applied to more areas of IT. Some of the common themes across all of these technologies are cost savings, flexibility, scalability, and simplified administration. Virtualization encompasses many technologies and types of technologies, but the family of virtualization technologies is growing as new things emerge, and as new uses are discovered for existing virtualization technologies.

Chapter 2: A Proposed Research Study

Richard Scroggins

Abstract

Trends in virtualization are always maturing, but choosing the right project on a limited budget can be a challenge. This problem is significant because IT managers are hesitant to adopt new technologies unless the ROI can be perceived to be justified. The ROI from virtualization technology projects has not been fully assessed. This leaves IT managers with a difficult decision as to which technology to invest their limited funds in. In this case you may be forced to do research to provide evidence that the investment is sound. The purpose of a research study would be to allow stakeholders to make more informed and scientifically based decisions regarding project choice and approval. This problem is significant because IT managers are hesitant to adopt new technologies unless the ROI can be perceived to be justified. The methodology for this study would be a Phenomenological Qualitative study that will collect data and explore the perception of ROI of server and desktop virtualization projects among IT managers. This study would consist of up to twenty participants or until data saturation is reached. In other words, at least twenty peers that you have contact information from that you know have been involved with a virtualization project. A manual process would be used to analyze the data to identify themes. The manual process will allow for the grouping and association of terms and themes between interview documents. Common terms and themes will be assigned codes to detect the presence of similarities between the interviews. This information can be documented within a spreadsheet for presentation to stakeholders. The following is a mock research proposal in the academic style.

Statement of the Problem

Trends in virtualization are always maturing, but choosing the right project on a limited budget can be a challenge. This problem is significant because IT managers are hesitant to adopt new technologies unless the ROI can be perceived to be justified. The ROI from virtualization technology projects has not been fully assessed. This leaves IT managers with a difficult decision as to which technology to invest their limited funds in.

Purpose of the Study

The purpose of the research is to allow stakeholders to make more informed and scientifically based decisions regarding project choice and approval.

Rationale

The strength of this study is that it will collect real data; however, the limitation is that it requires the participation of IT managers from external organization. This sampling method will be more precise and have a higher rate of success that random sampling. My role as the researcher is to collect this data from a population of individuals that I have worked with, or met in the past. This should provide good result, as long as bias is not introduced.

Research Questions

What are the perceptions of ROI between past server and desktop virtualization technology projects among IT Managers?

Significance of the Study

This problem is significant because IT managers are hesitant to adopt new technologies unless the ROI can be perceived to be justified.

Qualitative Research

I would be using a quantitative method for collecting most types of information from IT, rather than a qualitative. With a qualitative approach you will get user opinions and firsthand accounts of whatever you are looking at, but you may not get quantifiable data. Day (1997) says "While some research methods are well suited to addressing the who, what, when, and where of consumer behavior, the qualitative research course emphasizes methods that address the whys of behavior. And, while some research methods are useful for describing, explaining, and predicting consumer behavior, qualitative methods help achieve a better understanding of consumers " (p. 01). This problem exists in any scenario where you need quantifiable data, although, you might get a ball park estimate from interviews. In addition to asking questions about the process from a qualitative approach, you could ask questions about financial information and produce a ball park figure with some amount of accuracy given a statistical variance. Statistics can be very useful when you want to make a ball park prediction, and this might be enough for many scenarios. Ann (1998) again makes the case for the limitation of the qualitative approach when applied to data that needs to be quantified. According to Ann (1998), "Both forms of qualitative work look for details about preferences, motivations, and actions that are not easily made numeric." (p. 01). Although I see value in the qualitative approach for some aspects of IT research, I see it as being limited in the ability to provide the solid numbers that are usually needed to justify a project. Computer Scientists and IT Managers and rarely moved to action by feelings. There are many opportunities and choices in the Qualitative research direction.

There are also many in the Quantitative research direction, as well, but Qualitative research is our focus here. For my proposed study, since I am using a small group of about 20, I think, thus far, that the Delphi method is most appropriate for my proposed study. The Delphi method is a structured communication technique, originally developed as a systematic, interactive forecasting method which relies on a panel of experts. The experts answer questionnaires in two or more rounds. After each round, a facilitator provides an anonymous summary of the experts' forecasts from the previous round as well as the reasons they provided for their judgments. Thus, experts are encouraged to revise their earlier answers in light of the replies of other members of their panel. Grisham (2009) describes using the Delphi method to great effect, "The Delphi approach is one of many that may be selected for researching PM issues and problems. It is appropriate for researching complex issues where larger scale quantitative "hard data" fails to unearth richness in tacit knowledge to help the research understand subtle expert opinion. It does not offer the rigor of clinical testing or quantitative analysis, but it provides a scientific methodology that is well suited to issues that require the insights of subject matter experts." (p. 1). This analysis of the subject matter experts is what I am most after in my proposed study.

However, I think that the best complement for my proposed Phenomenological study is the exploratory inquiry. Given the idea that the Phenomenological method is focused on extracting new Phenomena from interviews, pairing this with the exploratory inquiry technique should produce the best results. Exploratory research is research that conducted for a problem that has not been clearly defined. Exploratory research helps determine the best research design, data collection method and selection of subjects. It should not draw definitive conclusions. Exploratory inquiry is very valuable when research on the topic is limited. Lehning (2013) states, "This exploratory qualitative inquiry added to a limited body of research on the topic of community college presidents who practice the servant leadership philosophy, their influence on organizational effectiveness, and their influence on creating benefits for their community. The research question directing this study asked, what are the practices, experiences, organizational effects, obstacles, and benefits of the servant leadership practice of community college presidents in a southern state?" (p. 1). Additionally, this method will complement my proposed Phenomenological study by helping to translate the lived experiences of the study participants, which is at the core of my proposed study. On the subject of lived experiences of the study participants, Lehning (2013) states, "An exploratory qualitative inquiry was used to document the lived experiences of 15 community college presidents in a southern state who practice servant leadership philosophy, their effectiveness, their ability to overcome the obstacles to servant leadership practice, and the benefits." (p. 1).

Qualitative Observation is both related to the reading, and something that I used specifically for this post by performing qualitative observations at my weekly IT staff meeting this morning. I observed the interactions between staff members and the repeatable and individual mannerisms of individuals. Qualitative observations are related to characteristics of what is being observed, contrasted with Quantitative observations, which have to do with things that can be precisely measured. My main objective in using Qualitative observations in the meeting was to observe the attitude of each staff member towards the projects that they were assigned, and to see how their tone of voice and mannerisms affected the mode of the IT manager. I observed that positive acceptance was met with a positive attitude and the negative acceptance was met with a negative attitude. DeRosia & Christensen (2009), used Qualitative observations effectively and noted their results, "The technique introduces a method to test a priori hypotheses using qualitative, emergent observation and analysis without the biasing influence of prior knowledge of the hypotheses being tested." (p. 1).

Existing data can be an excellent source of research data. Researchers often analyze data that they did not collect. Existing data may be data sets, but may also be interview notes or audio or video sources. There is one ethical concern with using existing data. If data were collected for research purposes, the original agreement with the subjects must have included permission for identifiable data to be shared with other researchers. Within their study, O'Callaghan, Soboleva, & Barratt (2010) found existing data to be of use and noted the following, “While risk assessment must be rigorous, new approaches are necessary to improve the efficiency of the process. Utilization of published information and existing data on the phenology and population dynamics of test species in the field can be combined with limited amounts of experimental biosafety data to predict possible outcomes on species persistence.” (p. 1).

Qualitative Interviews, is a method that ties directly to my proposed Phenomenological study. For my proposed study, since I am using a small group of about 20, direct and in person Qualitative Interviews will be used. “Interviews are among the most familiar strategies for collecting qualitative data. The different qualitative interviewing strategies in common use emerged from diverse disciplinary perspectives resulting in a wide variation among interviewing approaches.

Unlike the highly structured survey interviews and questionnaires used in epidemiology and most health services research, we examine less structured interview strategies in which the person interviewed is more a participant in meaning making than a conduit from which information is retrieved." (Dicicco-Bloom & Crabtree, 2006, p. 1). Frels & Onwuegbuzie (2013), state the following regarding qualitative interviews, "the qualitative interview process enhances interpretations by helping researchers better contextualize qualitative findings" (p. 1). This is very relevant and well suited for the purposes of my proposed study.

Another approach used in qualitative studies is keyword analysis, which identifies information through keywords. Kevork & Vrechopoulos (2009), who used keyword analysis to study CRM, commented on the subject, "In the present paper, we follow a quite different approach for the identification of the CRM research areas. Specifically, we use as the sole criterion of classification the keywords reported in the articles (in fact keywords expressions) together with their frequencies. The authors' keywords are taken as an authentic indicator about the articles' subject areas. In this sense, the keywords are one of the most revealing characteristics about an article's content." (p. 1). The second analysis method chosen was meta-coding. Meta-coding, according to Hung & Low

(2008), " was chosen as the technique since it is recommended for identifying more abstract themes and produces a limited number of large meta-themes" (p. 1).

Research Design

The methodology for this study is a Phenomenological Qualitative study that will collect data and explore the perception of ROI of server and desktop virtualization projects among IT managers. The research design is that of a Phenomenological Qualitative study using the following steps of the Modified Van Kaam method by Moustakas (1994):

1.Listing and preliminary grouping: Every expression relevant to the experience should be listed.

2.Reduction and elimination: Determine the invariant constituents and identify those elements that are fundamental to the experience. These are analyzed with regard to two criteria:

a. Does the expression contain a moment of the experience that is necessary and sufficient for understanding the phenomenon?

b. Can it be extracted and labeled?

3.Clustering and thematizing the invariant constituents: This step results in clustering the constituents into themes and labeling them, forming the core themes of the experience.

4. Validation: The invariant constituents are checked against the complete transcription of each participant to ensure that they are expressed explicitly in the transcription. They should be compatible with what is contained in the transcription; if incompatible, they are irrelevant and should be discarded.

5. Construction of a textural description using the themes and invariant constituents for each participant, including verbatim examples.

6.Construction of a structural description of the experience based on the textural description and imaginative variation.

7. Construction of a composite textural description that integrates all of the individual textural descriptions into a universal textural description.

8.Construction of a composite structural description that integrates all of the individual structural descriptions into a universal structural description.

9.Finally, synthesize the composite textural and composite structural descriptions into an integrated whole that captures the meanings and essences of the experience for the group as a whole.

Sample

This study will consist of up to twenty participants or until data saturation is reached. Participants will be from within the Houston, Dallas, and Austin Texas technology triangle. A manual process will be used to analyze the data to identify themes. The manual process will allow for the grouping and association of terms and themes between interview documents. Common terms and themes will be assigned codes to detect the presence of similarities between the interviews.

Setting

The setting will be varied based on the availability of each participant.

Instrumentation/Measures

Research Questions:

1) What types of virtualization project did you or your company undertake?

2) Were you a project stakeholder or technical asset on the project?

3) Were you involved in all aspects of the project, or a subset?

4) How concerned were you about success during the project?

5) Would you advise another group to undertake the same type of project?

6) What one thing would you change about your project?

7) Do you consider your virtualization project to be successful?

8) Do you perceive to have received a positive ROI from your virtualization project?

Data Collection

Interviews will be conducted in person with follow up meeting facilitated by phone, e-mail, or various social media methods. A manual process will be used to analyze the data to identify themes. The manual process will allow for the grouping and association of terms and themes between interview documents. Common terms and themes will be assigned codes to detect the presence of similarities between the interviews. The best complement for my proposed Phenomenological study is the exploratory inquiry. Given the idea that the Phenomenological method is focused on extracting new Phenomena from interviews, pairing this with the exploratory inquiry technique should produce the best results. Exploratory research is research that conducted for a problem that has not been clearly defined. Exploratory research helps determine the best research design, data collection method and selection of subjects. Qualitative Interviews, is a method that ties directly to my proposed Phenomenological study. For my proposed study, since I am using a small group of about 20, direct and in person Qualitative Interviews will be used.

Validity and Reliability

This design is based on an established design by Sneed (2006). "Interviews are among the most familiar strategies for collecting qualitative data. The different qualitative interviewing strategies in common use emerged from diverse disciplinary perspectives resulting in a wide variation among interviewing approaches. Unlike the highly structured survey interviews and questionnaires used in epidemiology and most health services research, we examine less structured interview strategies in which the person interviewed is more a participant in meaning making than a conduit from which information is retrieved." (Dicicco-Bloom & Crabtree, 2006, p. 1). Frels & Onwuegbuzie (2013), state the following regarding qualitative interviews, "the qualitative interview process enhances interpretations by helping researchers better contextualize qualitative findings" (p. 1). This is very relevant and well suited for the purposes of my proposed study. The Modified Van Kaam method by Moustakas (1994) is well established as a method for Phenomenological Qualitative studies. I see the Phenomenological method as being very useful. In my study, I am using it to look at perception, surrounding a particular IT theme.

Ethical Considerations

What is ethical and what is legal are not always the same. Unfortunately many of our laws are actually written by lobbyist, and their motives are not always ethical. Also what is ethical varies widely by culture. However, most of our core laws are based on a common core morality. Depending on what business you are in, there could be many legal ramifications of a network or data outage that causes loss of critical business to customers. If you were a service provider and your outage impacted other businesses and their ability to conduct their business, you might be liable for any loss of revenue. Given the advantages of virtualization in the area of disaster recovery, choices on whether or not to virtualize can have a significant impact on the future of an organization. This is another reason why the research questions in this study are important to the overall success of an organization. Additionally, the ethical implications in not providing back-up or disaster recovery for you organization or customers might show negligence. If negligence is proved, it might be easier for someone to get a judgment against you or your company. In a case of gross negligence, you might have a scenario like the company Enron, where some employees might go to prison. Although the ultimate goal of many businesses may be profit, it has to be achieved in an ethical manner. Whether you are complying with industry regulations, or just doing your best to protect your employees and customers.

Chapter 3: Transforming IT Management

Introduction

Weill and Ross (2008) describe IT governance as a messy process, "IT governance can be messy, but good governance arrangements enable individuals representing an enterprises conflicting goals to reconcile their views to the enterprise's benefit." (p. 1). This is a process that must involve the CIO or highest ranking IT manager. This is one area where the role of the CIO has changed over time, to share a role in governance with others in upper management. On the issue of true IT governance and best practices, the CIO plays the principle role. The CIO must understand the expectations of the management team and also know the limitations of the IT resources and how best to meet the management teams needs within existing or available limitations or capabilities. I see IT governance as a function of structure or procedure that is related to organizational structure. Following a set of best practices would help Alcon. (Dube, Bernier, & Roy, 2009) Best practices is a term that has a wide availability of interpretations. Best practices are usually a set of configuration guidelines from a manufacturer or high level users group. It is also common to find different sets of best practices from different sources. IT governance is a critical factor in establishing the right IT-business alignment and for meeting the needs of high level stakeholders. This has an effect on the performance of an organization and is critical to that organization meeting its mission or goals. Another major aspect of the CIO role that has changed over time due to legal and cultural changes is the contribution to IT and corporate policies. These policies can cover a broad range of topics, from the use of thumb drives and burners to the acceptable use of corporate computers. These policies will be different in each company based on their values and circumstances. An acceptable use policy is one that is very common in most companies and may govern things like the ability to listen to music at work; this is one that might be a coordinating effort between the CIO and the HR Manager. This policy might be affected by the company's internet connection speed, which if slow might restrict the use of online music. Companies also might not want music stored on hard drives or servers for space or legal reasons. All these things and many more are factors that the modern CIO must evaluate when drafting or contributing to policies and this is an issue that can get very deep. Overall, I thing that the position of CIO is one that is far more improved and respected than it once was, to spite the complications that come with the job. I also believe that this trend will continue in the same direction in the future as the CIO role will take on more and more strategic importance in the company and corporation of tomorrow.

Informal or undocumented governance is acceptable in an IT organization for many functions that are not directly related to high level project components or management tasks. Such informal governance can include tasks that the CIO or IT Manager may perform as part of the unspoken portions of the job. One role that I think that it important of any CIO or IT Manager is that of leading and inspiring the IT department. This may include providing leadership and direction, or maintaining a high level of moral. One way to keep moral high may be by providing newer equipment; most IT employees like to use and play with the latest toys and have good equipment for everyday use. Another way might be in providing occasional team building activities, like a weekly lunch or monthly activities that the department does together. Communications to the group and keeping everyone in the loop to company changes is also important. Treating everyone with respect and letting them know that they are doing a good job and contributing. Also, the CIO has to function as a buffer between upper management and IT department employees for many things, like programming or support issues, or corporate policies that effect the IT department. Basically, the CIO is in a position to look out, so to speak, for the people in their department, and their interests. (Weill & Ross, 2009) This also includes managing the expectations of the upper management group. I am not necessarily suggesting that the IT department is exempt from IT policies, but there is room for stretching policies within the IT department and the CIO should understand that.

My company has an established a governance format that applies to all sections and departments of the company. The governance format or archetype that we use is a Business Monarchy backed up by the ISO 9001 standard. This standard is defined by Wikipedia
(n.d) as "The ISO 9000 family of standards is related to quality management systems and designed to help organizations ensure that they meet the needs of customers and other stakeholders while meeting statutory and regulatory requirements related to the product. The standards are published by ISO, the International Organization for Standardization, and available through National standards bodies. ISO 9000 deals with the fundamentals of quality management systems, including the eight management principles on which the family of standards is based. ISO 9001 deals with the requirements that organizations wishing to meet the standard have to fulfill. Third party certification bodies provide independent confirmation that organizations meet the requirements of ISO 9001. Over a million organizations worldwide are independently certified, making ISO 9001 one of the most widely used management tools in the

world today." (p. 01). Sandford (2006) details the value of the ISO 9000 family, "ISO 9001 describes a basic, effective quality management system (QMS). Compliance to its requirements is the starting point toward achieving excellence in an organization. ISO 9001 compliant QMS can act as the first steps toward excellence." (p. 01). The ISO 9000 family of standards is the world leader in standardization of processes and value chain management. On the reasons behind the widespread use, Wikipedia (n.d) says, "The global adoption of ISO 9001 may be attributable to a number of factors. A number of major purchasers require their suppliers to hold ISO 9001 certification. In addition to several stakeholders' benefits, a number of studies have identified significant financial benefits for organizations certified to ISO 9001." (p.01). A 2011 survey from the British Assessment Bureau showed that 44% of certified clients had won new business since gaining certification. (ISO 9001 proven to help win new business, 2001) This is used to establish competitive advantage in our industry and the structure of our company is molded around this standard. Organizational structure is definitely influenced by the economy and industry trends. My current company used to have a standard departmental structure, but now we refer to everything at that level as a process and groups have been reorganized along process lines. As such, we have process owners and process champions instead of managers and supervisors; however individuals may be part of multiple processes within the organization. We call the IT department "Managing Information Services" for instance. These choices affected our organizational structure and in turn the global organization because we are a worldwide company. Trends set in the western culture, where most businesses are based effect businesses in those countries and then it ripples around the world. These two structure, what I consider the traditional model and then the process model each have their own pros and cons. The traditional model is more common and can new employees or within a relationship with another company. This is a real concern, because we make a lot of acquisitions and the process based structure has a steep learning curve. The process based model appears more complex to the outsider, but in reality is more streamlined and efficient. Economic challenges are a partial driver for us in adapting to the process based structure initially and the ISO 9001 standard, and they affect virtually all businesses. This is because even in a good economy, every business must seek optimum efficiency and profit. This is even more critical in lean time like the global economy is currently experiencing.

I think that the alignment between business and IT is identified by the performance of the business and the commitment to IT. I also see the position of CIO or IT Manager as the central figure in measuring this. One reason to measure this is to see where the business is headed and if you will be able to respond to future change and be successful in the future. The role of the CIO has changed dramatically over the last few decades. (Chun & Mooney, 2009) This is something that I have seen firsthand over the course of my own career, in fact. I my company, the CIO role actually manages the technology and strategic use of IT for two sister companies. I have seen the business or functional groups grow more and more dependent on the IT department and the CIO for not just technology, but also strategic business direction and process design. The modern IT department seems to be seen as a corporate brain trust. I see that businesses rely on IT and the CIO role far more than they used to, and that is fine as long as proper boundaries are maintained. The IT department and IT resources represent a large part of any modern business and are justified by large savings for the business in money and manpower. I know that this was not always the case. A few decades ago the IT department was seen as not needed at all, then as a necessary evil. I worked in company just a decade ago that still had older executives that saw the IT department as just that, a marginally necessary evil. Today, it is a foregone conclusion for any executive or business student that the IT department will play a large role in any company at least of medium size. So this is progress for sure, that allows the modern IT department and CIO to have a place of honor, purpose, and great responsibility. Also, the CIO has to function as a buffer between upper management and IT department employees for many things, like programming or support issues, or corporate policies that effect the IT department. Basically, the CIO is in a position to look out, so to speak, for the people in their department, and their interests. This also includes managing the expectations of the upper management group. Another major aspect of the CIO role that has changed over time due to legal and cultural changes is the contribution to IT and corporate policies. These policies can cover a burners to the acceptable use of corporate computers. These policies will be different in each company based on their values and circumstances. An acceptable use policy is one that is very common in most companies and may govern things like the ability to listen to music at work; this is one that might be a coordinating effort between the CIO and the HR Manager. This policy might be affected by the company's internet connection speed, which if slow might restrict the use of online music. Companies also might not want music stored on hard drives or servers for space or legal reasons. All these things and many more are factors that the modern CIO must evaluate when drafting or contributing to policies and this is an issue that can get very deep. Overall, I thing that the position of CIO is one that is far more improved and respected than it once was, to spite the complications that come with the job. I also believe that this trend will continue in the same direction in the future as the CIO role will take on more and more strategic importance in the company and corporation of tomorrow. As far as relating to IT portfolio management, this is just another role of the CIO and part of the IT/business alignment.

Chapter 4: Strategic Management Theories

Introduction

The goal of this chapter is to compare and contrast contemporary strategic management theories. Additionally, the secondary goal is to evaluate the implications for strategic information technology management. Management of people is the direct control of human motivation and behavior. Human motivation, like behavior is complex, and a science unto itself. Human motivation theory seeks to understand human motivations, and therefore understand human behavior to a level such that predictions can be made. The study of human motivation has a background or base in physiological, behavioral, cognitive, and social sciences. However, those existing disciplines are not sufficient alone or combine to study this complex topic. The behaviors linked to human motivation are linked to very evolutionarily basic aspects of our biology, despite the advanced cognitive abilities of man. The ability to predict human motivation and behavior is very important to companies and organizations as they are always seeking new strategies to motivate and respond to the needs of their employees. This in turn makes the organization more efficient and can increase profits or success. Human motivation theories or strategies can be classified in one of several types: humanistic motivation, arousal motivation, instinct motivation, incentive motivation, or drive motivation. Each category of motivation theory or strategy presents value as well as challenges. In the overall process of increasing job satisfaction and commitment within the IT department, human motivation is necessary, but choosing the most appropriate strategy is difficult. Therefore, each human motivation theory or strategy must be researched and examined in detail to understand the value and individual challenges presented. Only then, can the best fit be made and an appropriate human motivation strategy be chosen and applied to the IT department. Additionally any independent challenges that are motivation theory agnostic must also be evaluated and presented as part of the research. This will allow for the creation of a complete human motivation implementation strategy that extends beyond the basics of theory.

Theories of motivation

Humanistic theories of motivation propose that human motivation and behavior are based on cognitive function. The principal theory in this category is Maslow's hierarchy of needs, which was discussed briefly in the previous section. Maslow's theory outlines five basic needs: physiological, safety, belongingness or love, esteem, and self-actualization. These needs are presented as hierarchical, meaning that higher needs will not manifest until lower need are met. Physiological needs are the most basic, and include the need for such things are air, water, or food. Security needs include safety and security. Job safety and security are important needs to employees and should be considered when evaluating basic human motivation in the effort to form a motivation strategy within business. Social needs include love and affection, but also belonging. The sense of belonging, or inclusion in groups or projects could be an important factor in job satisfaction and commitment in IT departments. Esteem needs include self-esteem, personal worth, social recognition, and accomplishment. These needs definitely translate to business in terms of salary, promotion, and recognition. Finally, self-actualizing needs are the highest level of needs and are more self-focused, including things like lifetime achievement or just fully realizing ones potential (Maslow, 1943). Can this theory actually be directly applied to business or the IT department? To this point, Cao, Jiang, Oh, Li, Liao, and Chen (2013) write, "With respect to Maslow's hierarchy of needs theory, we found that social needs and self-actualization needs are particularly relevant in capturing the motivations of SNSs." (p. 170). This is core to this research, that a theory developed to study human motivations can be used and expanded to fit a particular subset of humans, that being those within a business or IT department. More than simply adapting the theory or model, but using it to create a human motivation strategy that can be used not only to predict, but also respond to factors like job satisfaction, success, and commitment.

Arousal theories of motivation propose that a person's behavior is linked to a need or desire to increase or decrease their level of arousal. By participating in tasks that are either exciting or relaxing a person is able to regulate their level of arousal. This class of theories would not seem, on the surface, to apply directly to the business or IT environments, but the Yerkes-Dodson law suggests a direct relationship between arousal level and performance. According to the theory, increased arousal, to a point of diminishing return, can improve performance. Also, it suggests that there is an optimal level of arousal or stress that varies from person to person or from task to task. The theory suggests that this is partially due to stress providing focus (Yerkes & Dodson, 1908). Using this concept to increase job satisfaction and commitment, however, is a different matter. Increasing performance or focus through the application or reduction of stress by a manager may very well lead to increased performance, but a stressful environment is unlikely to increase job satisfaction or commitment. This is far more likely to lead to an increase in burn out and turn over. This theory is widely used. Palethorpe and Wilson (2011) write,

“The Yerkes-Dodson law has been widely adopted in numerous forms.” (p. 420). While the concept of arousal may be linked to business and performance, it does not appear to be useful as part of any strategy that would increase job satisfaction and commitment in IT departments unless it is approached from the stress reduction perspective or maintaining an environment where the stress is below the optimal line describes by the Yerkes-Dodson law.

Instinct theories propose that human behavior is based on evolutionary programming, genetics, and heredity. Just like birds migrate based on instinct, humans likewise behave based on instinct according to this idea. According to this theory, all life forms are born with innate, biology based tendencies that favor survival. Instincts in this case are behavior patterns that are not based on learning or experience (Melucci, 2010). "Instinct theory proposes that organisms engage in certain behaviors because they lead to success in terms of natural selection. Instinct theory casts motivation as essentially intrinsic and biologically based. Migration and mating are examples of instinctually motivated behavior in animal." (Melucci, 2010, p. 232) While it can be clearly shown that lower animals engage in instinctive patterns of behavior, this is difficult to show in humans, due to the difficulty in separating these supposed instincts from learned behavior or actions based on life experience. Humans do have observable instincts, such as the suckling instinct, or the instinct to hold your breath under water. The challenge for this research is how this theory can be used to analyze job satisfaction and commitment in IT departments. Complex behaviors like the tendency to stay with a company or leave may be difficult to tie directly to instinct. To be classified as an instinct, a behavior must be shown to exist as a pattern within an entire species, however most psychologist view human behaviors as being rooted in both physiological and psychological factors (Myers, 2011). So while instinct may exists in humans and have some control over behavior, is not significant enough. Neither has it been sufficiently shown to be the driving force such that a human motivation strategies could be built based on instinct for business purposes. While such factors as safety and security might have a biological origin and have a role in job satisfaction and commitment in IT departments, the Instinct theory of motivation is simply not a logical tool for this type of research.

Incentive theories of motivation suggest that human motivation is connected to rewards. One example of a reward that is directly linked to business is the motivation to work in exchange for the reward of a paycheck. Additionally, the theory is expanded to take reinforcement into account, in other words after the cycle of work and pay is repeated a number of times the motivation will be stronger. To apply this in principle, a reward would be given after a desired action occurred assuming that because of this the behavior would be repeated. This would associate positive meaning to the behavior. Repetition of this action and reward cycle would, according to the theory result in the concept of reinforcement and form a habit. Incentive theory can be further divided into two sub categories: intrinsic incentive motivation theory and extrinsic incentive motivation theory motivation. In intrinsic incentive motivation theory, motivation is theorized to come from one's own self. In extrinsic incentive motivation theory, motivation is theorized to come from an external source or person. The incentive theory of motivation is supported directly by the work of B.F. Skinner, where he stresses the importance of external influence. Skinner suggests that if a person's actions are received positively by others, that those actions are likely to be repeated. The opposite is also proposed that negative reception will likely lead to that behavior not occurring again (Skinner, 1978). The link between motivation and pay is also very strong. Kunz and Quitman (2011) write, "The relationship between extrinsic incentives and intrinsic motivation has attracted much debate over the last decades. Most of the extant literature focuses on the effect of different types of incentives, particularly the role of monetary rewards for intrinsic motivation." (p. 55). The overall concept of the incentive theory of motivation appears to provide a good theoretical framework with which to create a concise human motivation strategy for business and the IT department to analyze and increase job satisfaction and commitment in IT departments.

The drive theory of human motivation suggests that behavior is linked to internal desires to reduce tension related to biological needs. This would include eating to reduce the internal stress cause by hunger. This theory is strongest when attempting to account for base biological needs like hunger or thirst, but does not account for such behaviors completely, as it does not explain overeating, which is not directly related to hunger. The drive theory was principally introduced by Clark Hull, and has been further developed over time. As with other theories, the concept of reinforcement, caused by the reduction of stress or drive, is central. Reinforcement increases the likelihood that the same behaviors will continue to manifest (Hull, 1935). "In order to survive in its environment, an organism must behave in ways that meet these survival needs. When survival is in jeopardy, the organism is in a state of need (when the biological requirements for survival are not being met) so the organism behaves in a fashion to reduce that need." (Hull, 1935, p. 491) This theory has been criticized for not identifying or accounting for secondary contributors or reinforcers of behavior. Also, many people participate willingly in activities that increase stress, such as dangerous activities like fighting or racing. This theory's lack to completely explain behavior makes it an unlikely candidate for use in this motivation research. There is very little or nothing at all from this theory that can be used to build a complete human motivation strategy to analyze or to increase job satisfaction and commitment in IT departments. The only obvious value to this theory is the place in history as a theory that was used to develop other theories, such as Maslow's hierarchy of needs, the principle humanistic theory of human motivation, which emerged as an alternative to Hull's theory.

Success Factors of motivation strategies

Motivation can be defined as an innate or internal condition that encourages or causes a person to act. This action is called behavior, and this behavior is often repeated in patterns called habits. The study of human motivation seeks to define and uncover this, while human motivation strategies are defined to control it. There are many factors and challenges in creating a successful human motivation strategy. Something that qualifies as both is making sure that any particular human motivation strategy is based on a solidly supported theory of human motivation. In the case of this research, the incentive theory of human motivation is well supported and exemplifies the theoretical basic of a complete human motivation strategy and overall research strategy. In the case of using the incentive theory, the strategy employed must address incentive. One major incentive related to job satisfaction and commitment in IT departments is pay or compensation. The core motivation theory will help to identify why this factor is important. In other words, does having financial security satisfy base or biological needs and create an employee that is stress free and can commit to the organization? Another factor in developing a complete human motivation strategy is accounting for all of the factors that affect motivation, beyond those identified by the core theory of human motivation used. Achievement is an important factor to consider and measure. Other factors include appreciation, freedom, management style or pressure, environment, social interaction, flexibility, access to technology, growth opportunity, and clear goals among many others. Any complete human motivation strategy must address all of these factors that affect the interaction between the business and the employee, but especially those that directly affect job satisfaction and commitment.

Job satisfaction is a very complex concept that represents a level of satisfaction with one's job or employment. Satisfaction is based on a multiple factors that will vary on a person by person basis. This is a very qualitative concept and relies on personal feelings and opinion to represent or collect data on. This may vary significantly between person of different age, gender, profession, geographic location, etc. Although job satisfaction is a multifaceted concept, the aspects of job satisfaction can still be linked to basic human motivations. Researchers divide job satisfaction measurements into two categories: affective job satisfaction, or cognitive job satisfaction. Feelings about the job describe affective job satisfaction, while thoughts about the job describe cognitive job satisfaction. It is also to differentiate between job satisfaction and job performance or job commitment. Studies indicate that there is no direct relationship between these concepts. A person may be motivated to perform a task by any number of factors and still not be satisfied with needing to do it. Likewise, a person may be very satisfied with their job and not perform to the level expected by management. Furthermore neither of these, job satisfaction or performance, directly relate to commitment. Therefore it is a very complex relationship between the factors of job satisfaction and the motivations that influence job performance and commitment that provide the complete picture. Ram (2013) writes, "In this age of specialization, motivating a worker and providing him with the much needed job satisfaction is extremely important to enable him to realize his true potential and worth to the organization. It is therefore important to explain the relationship between job satisfaction and job performance." (p. 16). The research suggests that there are four main influences that combine to contribute to satisfaction, performance, and commitment: environment, communication, employee recognition, and aspects of the individual. The aspects of the individual can be further broken down into the following: emotion, genetics, personality, and psychology. The complex challenge that organizations face in trying to increase job satisfaction and commitment in IT departments is to develop a strategy that addresses all of the influences. Fortunately these challenges can be mitigated with the use of one of several established job satisfaction and commitment models.

Job satisfaction models

One very prominent job satisfaction model is the range of affect theory. This model looks at the difference between what a person wants and what they have. Satisfaction is determined by evaluating this discrepancy. Job satisfaction is broken down into job facets. Changes to any facet of satisfaction can improve or reduce job satisfaction. The model also suggests that a person will most likely value one facet of their job more than the others. For any detailed and accurate analysis of job satisfaction, you must identify what job factor is important (Locke, 1976). This could be done through a survey question. Carmeli, Elizur, and Yaniv (2007) write, "Facet analysis provides an important tool for researchers to understand the structure of work commitment. The multifaceted approach employed in this study enabled the designing and empirical testing of a structural definitional framework of work commitment." (p. 638). Identifying and responding to the individual facets of job satisfaction is important and is a challenge in trying to increase job satisfaction and commitment in IT departments. Therefore it must be incorporated into the organizational strategy.

The dispositional approach is another job satisfaction model. Like the affect theory, the dispositional approach suggests that job satisfaction is based largely on the individual. The theory also suggests that job satisfaction tends to be stable in an individual over their entire career. This, per the theory, suggests that people have an innate disposition and a tendency to maintain a particular level of job satisfaction. The dispositional approach suggests that there are four self-evaluations that determine job satisfaction: self-esteem, self-efficacy, locus of control, and neuroticism (Staw, Bell, & Clausen, 1986). Zhai, Lindorff, and Cooper (2013) write, "Examining the mechanisms underlying dispositions and job satisfaction are important, as they attempt to explain how and why dispositions affect job satisfaction and to what extent theories such as the dispositional model of job satisfaction are supported empirically." (p. 543). While the dispositional approach has support and merit, the focus may be too limited to individuals, however, a model focused on the individual alone might be well suited for a research study using a survey instrument. This model may serve as a model to analyze job satisfaction and commitment in IT departments.

Equity theory is based on the idea that a person balances input and output and seeks an equitable relationship, to which job satisfaction is based. According to the theory, a person will balance the things gained with the things given and make up a ratio. They will then compare their ratio to what they perceive someone else's is to decide if they think that they are being treated equitably. This equity is subject to change as well, if the parameters change. In other words if the person being compared against gets a raise, there will be an imbalance. The theory identifies three types of people: benevolent, equity sensitive, and entitled. The benevolent person is satisfied even when under rewarded. The equity sensitive person believes that everyone should be rewarded equally. Finally, the entitled person believes that they are due anything that they receive and more (Adams, 1965). This shows a potential connection between the perception of inequity and effort or commitment. Khalifa (2011) writes, "Research has been consistently showing a positive relationship between perception of equity and job satisfaction." (p. 130). This path of study or research has potential for uncovering factors that affect job satisfaction and commitment in IT departments. In terms of using a survey instrument, this model would suffice, provided the participants can be grouped according to their equity sensitivity level.

Discrepancy theory relates job satisfaction to anxiety. When performance and achievement are not met, anxiety builds up. Over time, an individual will learn the aspects of their job. When they fail to perform an aspect correctly, punishment is often the result. This understanding of punishment for failure results in agitation when obligations and responsibilities are not met. Also, if the obligations and responsibilities are met, then rewards like praise or approval are expected. Where the employer has real impact on job satisfaction, according to this is when the opposite employer reaction is present. In other words, if the obligations and responsibilities are met by the individual and punishment is given, job satisfaction will be negatively impacted (Higgins, 1987). Explaining the theory, Siddiqui and Saba (2013) write, "It means that if the actual outcomes of the employees are matched with the expected outcomes then their satisfaction level would be high but if the actual outcomes are lower than the expected one then the satisfaction level will be low." (p. 42). This concept may be difficult to factor into this research on job satisfaction and commitment in IT departments within the parameters of a survey instrument.

The two-factor theory, also called the motivator-hygiene theory, is a job satisfaction model created by Frederick Herzberg. According to the theory, job satisfaction and dissatisfaction are driven by different factors: motivation and hygiene. Motivations, in this case are things like recognition, promotion, raises, challenging work, etc. Hygiene, in this case means working conditions, company policies, supervisory action, job security, fringe benefits, etc. This theory suggests that to improve perceptions of job satisfaction, employers must focus on both aspects of motivation and hygiene. This means understanding which category a job factor exists in, whether it leads to satisfaction or dissatisfaction, and responding accordingly. This could be thought of as ensuring that an employee is satisfied, while at the same time, ensuring that they are not dissatisfied (Herzberg, 1964). In explaining the theory in detail, Tillman, Smith, and Tillman write:

> The theory posits that hygiene factors must be present in the job before motivators are used to stimulate the individual. Thus, motivators are unavailable for use until the hygiene factors are in place. Herzberg' s needs are specifically job related and reflect some of the distinct features that people want from their work. (Tillman, Smith, & Tillman, 2010, p. 107)

While this theory has complexity, it also has a solid foundation to support research on job satisfaction and commitment in IT departments and serve as a model with which to build a strategy upon.

Finally, the job characteristics model is a widely used framework for studying job satisfaction. The job characteristics model, proposed by Hackman and Oldham, provides five core job characteristics: skill variety, task identity, task significance, autonomy, and feedback. These characteristics in turn impact three critical psychological states: experienced meaningfulness, experienced responsibility for outcomes, and knowledge of the actual results. These psychological states further influence four outcomes: job satisfaction, absenteeism, work motivation, and performance. The model provides a method for combining these elements to calculate a motivating potential score, or MPS, for any job. This score then predicts how likely a jobs is to impact an individual's satisfaction and performance based on attitude (Hackman & Oldham, 1976). Michailidis and Dracou (2011) expand on the theory, "The Job Characteristics Model suggests that high internal motivation can be promoted by designing jobs that include the five core job characteristics - Skill Variety, Task Identity, Task Significance, Autonomy and Feedback." (p. 228). Real potential exists with using the job characteristics model, not only in researching job satisfaction and commitment in IT departments, but also in producing results that can properly align jobs to maximize satisfaction and commitment.

Conclusion

In conclusion, after researching many human motivation strategies and job satisfaction models, many options are available for any potential research into how they link directly to management. While much of the research sources are older, this is because these sources are seminal, and core to the research. However, beyond simply facilitating easy research, the true desire is to produce research results that have an impact on IT departments. To do this requires the correct components as the basic for the overall research strategy. The best theories to do this based on the research are the job characteristics model combined with the incentive theory of motivation. These two theories are complementary and should correspond together well as part of the overall research plan and strategy. After analyzing the research, a gap emerges. Unlike other fields of study, no unified theory of job satisfaction was discovered. This unified theory of job satisfaction would be an important development in understanding job satisfaction and how to use that to develop a proper management strategy.

Chapter 5: Motivation and IT Project Success

Introduction

The goal of this chapter is to Compare and contrast the types of quantitative research approaches used to conduct studies on the relationship between motivation and IT project success. Additionally, the secondary goal is to Examine and discuss the issues of sampling, validity, reliability, and bias within these contexts. Wester, Borders, Boul, and Horton (2013) define research as, "An activity conducted to increase knowledge by systematically collecting, analyzing, and interpreting data to answer carefully formulated questions about publicly observable phenomena." (p. 280). Research is a critical part of the scientific method that allows our society and species to understand the world around us. Research can be divided into multiple categories. The two predominant research categories are qualitative and quantitative. Simply making the choice between quantitative and qualitative research is a challenge that deadlocks many research projects. Students struggle with this very dilemma, often changing the direction of their research multiple times before settling on a solid direction.

Although there is value in the qualitative approach for some aspects of IT research, challenges with this type of research are often presented by limiting the ability to provide solid numbers that are typically needed to justify a project. Ann (1998) makes the case for the limitation of the qualitative approach when applied to data that needs to be quantified. According to Ann (1998), "Both forms of qualitative work look for details about preferences, motivations, and actions that are not easily made numeric." (p. 162). Beyond the initial challenge quantitative research presents challenges that are specific. Quantitative research can be defined as the investigation of some phenomena through the use of statistical, mathematical, or numeric data and applying some computational, observational, or mathematical techniques to show a fundamental connection. This process typically follows the scientific method and involves some hypothesis to which a defining relational question will be evaluated and proven or disproven. The overall research design for quantitative research typically includes models, theories, hypotheses, instruments, methods, controls, variables, collection, and analysis.

Types of Quantitative Research Approaches

Determining the purpose of the research and creating a purpose statement is the primary challenge of performing quantitative research. Two examples of potential research methods for this type of study are exploratory research and descriptive research. Exploratory research would be useful to explore the topic and identify new insights, while descriptive research relies more on an existing body of scholarly work and statistical data. Exploratory research would better fit the goals of a study that is exploring questions that pertain to the impact of perceived IT project success. Exploratory research is research that explores something new. While typically used when a problem has not been clearly defined, exploratory research can be combined with a review of existing literature to satisfy all aspects of the research. In the case of the perception of IT project success, especially in the direct area of virtualization technology, exploration is needed, as the perceptions of success are not clearly known. Mansourian (2008) writes, "One of the most important and extensive stages of this study was the period of data collection and analysis. In this stage, the researcher sought to find the answer of the primary research questions through a systematic data collection and inductive analysis which ended up with reasonable answers to the primary questions." (p. 273). Questioning is exploring and that is the root of scientific study. By exploring and answering questions, you contribute knowledge, whether it is for all mankind, or just for a small population. Exploratory research suggests an area where a question needs to be answered through exploration. Exploratory research is often associated with qualitative research, as there is a qualitative nature to any answer given to any question posed or answered by a human. This is relative to our basic nature, but the statistical data collected can still be quantified and is thus appropriate for quantitative research. Quantitative research is narrow and specific, and is able to reduce a complex question to a single number or set of numbers.

From the purpose of the research comes the research purpose statement, which is central to the research. The purpose statement describes the controlling idea of the study. Although research purpose and purpose statements are common to both quantitative and qualitative research, they are very specific to each type of research. In quantitative research, the purpose statement includes variables that can be independent, dependent, mediating, moderating or control variables. Identifying variables is a very important process that is unique to quantitative research.

Additional elements of conducting quantitative research

Choosing an instrument for the collection of data is another challenge of conducting quantitative research. There are many instruments to evaluate and choose from and often they are proprietary or must be modified for the specific research purposes. Examples of potential instruments that relate to a study on the impact of perceived IT project success on future IT project decision making include the use of direct interviews, observations, or surveys. Direct interviews present a challenge in arranging and facilitating the large number of interviews needed to collect enough data for an accurate quantitative study and are more frequently associated with qualitative research. Observations, while very useful in most hard scientific research, are difficult to facilitate in this type of study. Directly observing project and IT managers would present logistical difficulties. An ideal option for a qualitative study of this manner is the use of an online survey tool.

Due to the maturing nature of technology and survey services such as Survey Monkey, online surveys have become increasing prevalent. Sproull and Kiesler (1986) looked at patterns by comparing paper and electronic questionnaires and found that respondents made fewer errors and submitted supplementary content along with their answers on the electronic submissions. Surveys have the ability to reach more participants with greater simplicity and at a lower expense. Surveys also provide quantifiable answers that can be analyzed using statistical testing. Like any quantitative instrument, the objectives of the instrument must be defined and the method of data analysis must be accounted for prior to creating or submitting the survey.

Analyzing the data is a fundamental challenge to quantitative research. Rabhi, Yao, and Guabtni (2012) write, "Data analysis is an important part of the scientific process." (p. 489). Although collected data is analyzed in both qualitative and quantitative research, quantitative research uniquely analyzes the data mathematically. One way to mitigate the challenge of analyzing data within a quantitative study is to take advantage of technology. The use of software programs like SPSS allow for the importing and manipulation of data. Statistical tests like T-tests or ANOVA tests can be run from within the program and the statistical output is given in report format. Bhunia (2013) writes, "SPSS consists of an integrated series of computer programs that facilitate the user to understand data from questionnaire surveys and other sources, to maneuver them in diverse traditions and to generate an extensive choice of statistical analyses and reports, together with documentation." (p. 154). The most important aspect of data analysis is ensuring that the question posed by the research is answered. In other words, the results of the analysis must support the goal of the research and ensure that the hypothesis is either proved to an acceptable margin or disproved. Before analysis is done, levels of measurement must be determined. Levels of measurement are categorized as nominal, ordinal, interval, and ratio.

These levels of measurement have a direct influence on the types of analysis that is done. An initial step in analyzing the data is to simply tabulate the results using frequency and percent distributions. This will provide an overview that can be used for more detailed analysis. The analysis must also be data driven. There are several data analysis techniques that can be used to interpret the data, some include: histograms, T-tests, F-tests, ANOVA tests, cross tabulation, correlation, linear regression, or text analytics. Regardless of the methods employed, ultimately, the data must be interpreted, conclusions must be drawn, and the research question must be answered. It must be ensured that no bias is present as well.

Synthesizing an appropriate quantitative research strategy

Beyond the above identified challenges, the process of synthesizing these challenges into one quantitative research strategy is a prodigious challenge. Evaluating the core question of the study allows this synthesizing process to begin. The core question is, what is the impact of perceived IT project success on future IT project decision making among IT managers? Data collection through the use of a survey will produce data that can be correlated based on age and gender. Correlations based on age will provide insights as to how different generations of IT managers perceive and define success within completed IT projects. Correlations based on gender will provide insights as to how IT managers of different genders perceive and define success within completed IT projects. Looking at age and gender together will provide deeper insights into how men and women of different generation define success within completed virtualization technology projects. While studying the effects of gender and age on new technology implementation Elizabeth, Al-Gahtani, & Hubona (2007) wrote, “Demographic variables (e.g. gender and age) that have been reported to be significant moderators of the influences of attitude, subjective norm and perceived behavioral control on behavioral intention” (p. 352). Correlating the data analysis by age and gender contributes to a larger impact on the IT managers; which are the target audience of the study. Beyond this primary audience this data correlation strategy will likewise provide a greater contribution to the field in general and advance the stream of research.

In determining the elements needed to synthesize an appropriate quantitative research strategy, a research problem must be defined through a research statement. The research statement is very important to the overall strategy. The exam question describes a study on the impact of perceived IT project success on future IT project decision making. This problem is significant because IT managers are hesitant to engage in new technology projects unless there is a clear motivation, or there is a perception that project will be successful. It therefore becomes a valid action to research a solution to this significant problem through the mechanism of an exploratory online survey, where the perceptions of past project success can be computed and analyzed mathematically. Once this is completed, it can be presented to the target audience and community at large. In order to achieve the best results for this scenario, a statistically valid random sample is appropriate. This will include a random selection of IT managers in the United States who have completed a past IT project. In addition to information directly related to the perception of the past success of IT projects, some additional demographic data will be collected. Most important of this additional data is the age and gender of each survey participant. Correlating the resultant data based on age and gender will benefit the study by providing a more rich and substantive result.

One important aspect of this research is the intended audience, that of IT Managers. IT managers are also the participants of the study on the impact of perceived IT project success on future IT project decision making. The initial plan might be to sample a smaller geographic area.

This, however, may prove too narrow for the sample results needed. In this case, the survey would be expanded to a larger geographic area. It is very important to the research that these participants be IT managers directly involved in past IT projects. The role of the IT manager has changed dramatically over the last few decades. Businesses and functional groups grow more and more dependent on the IT department and the IT manager for not just technology, but also strategic business direction and process design. The modern IT department is transforming into the role of a corporate brain trust in many companies thus giving the modern IT manger much more control over the direction of corporate spending and strategy, and make this research more directly relevant to the entire corporation and long term performance. Therefore, this research has a greater potential impact on the field and potentially a wider audience. Kharuddin, Ashhari, and Nassir (2010) write, "Prior researchers have shown that information system adoption did increased firms' performances and operations efficiency." (p. 28). Understanding your audience and the impact that the research has is a separate challenge and needs to be addressed, as it impacts decisions regarding the research strategy. One potential alternative to a quantitative research study might be a qualitative research study on the perception of IT project success. However, given the technical aspects of the subject and the reliance on hard data that IT managers demand, the audience drives the research to a quantitative study.

In creating or determining an appropriate quantitative research strategy for a study on the impact of perceived IT project success on future IT project decision making, the next critical element is a valid theoretical framework. This framework is made up of concepts and theories or statements that are a combination of preconceptions and what is drawn from the research. The theoretical framework is what will connect this research to the existing research and advance the stream of knowledge. A core theoretical element to a study on the impact of perceived IT project success on future IT project decision making is that there may be a significant relationship between the perceptions of IT managers who have performed past projects and the effect that this has on future IT project decision making. This can be evaluated many ways. How does the perception of one IT Manager effect the decision of another? What percentage of success is enough to make a new IT manager comfortable with a project? There are many potential questions from this research. When the data is correlated on age and gender, these questions have much more depth and potential meaning for the research and primary audience. Evaluating these questions allows for a deeper ability to evaluate the phenomena associated with the larger or more general question. The process of developing the full theoretical framework unfolds throughout the entire research process and comes from several aspects of the research. The research problem is the first building block of the theoretical framework. The research variables are another key to the overall theoretical framework. The literature review will also contribute greatly to the theoretical framework and will provide the answers to the research question. The purpose of the theoretical framework and these elements are to allow the specific data to be analyzed and interpreted from the specific viewpoint of the researcher.

Issues associated with research elements

Sampling, or the sampling plan, is a critical piece of the overall research strategy. Sampling is the process of selecting participants for your research. The plan for this study is to use a random sample of survey participants. A random sample is a basic type of probability sample. In order to draw a random sample, a population of interest is needed first. In the case of a study on the impact of perceived IT project success on future IT project decision making, the population of interest is IT managers within the United States. From this population of interest, a subset will be randomly selected through the use of an online survey tool. One issue with sampling is choosing the correct sampling plan for the study. A purposive sample was initially considered for this study, but the risk of bias was a concern. A random sample through the use of an online survey tool lowers the risk of bias. This also lowers the level of effort verses the use of a purposive sampling plan. The research strategy includes the plan to use the software program GPower to calculate the appropriate sample size for this study. GPower is an analysis program that performs analysis for many statistical tests such as T-tests or ANOVAS. This is very important to this study, as correlations will be tested and analyzed. In other words, the power represents the probability that the null hypothesis is correctly rejected. This is significant to sampling, because sampling size is a major factor in determining sampling error in any test result. Therefore, making sure that the sample size is large enough is critical to ensuring a large enough power rating for any statistical test that will be applied to the sample date collected. Given the correlation of the sample data in this study based on age and gender, multiple statistical tests will likely be required.

Reliability and validity are both important concepts in measuring and analyzing statistical data. They are, however slightly different. Reliability can be understood as consistency, where validity can be understood as accuracy. This is similar in concept to an archer or rifleman shooting at a target. Many shots placed in a small group would represent high consistency or reliability. This does not mean that those shots are placed near the bull's eye but only that they are near each other. Accuracy, opposed to this describes shots that are close to the bull's eye, but not necessarily close to any other shots. In terms of statistical analysis, validity is the concept that a test is measuring what it is designed to measure where reliability measures that a test shows results that are consistent. In order for a test to be considered proper, it must be both valid and reliable. Reliability does not imply validity, and conversely validity does not imply reliability, both must be independently established. Brown and Ki (2013) write:

> "Similar to other disciplines, including psychology and marketing, as future studies are conducted to measure these constructs, the gap between the need for better, more valid measures and the lack of these measures must be addressed to enhance empirical research. Reliable and valid scales should be adapted or created to measure these constructs as precisely as possible. Such measurement of constructs is an important component of all scientific research." (Brown & Ki, 2013, p. 363).

As stated, these concepts are important to scientific research in general. There are several types of statistical validity, but for this research, the most important is construct validity. Stated another way, in developing a complete and appropriate quantitative research strategy for a study on the impact of perceived IT project success on future IT project decision making, the determination must be made as to whether the tests do in fact measure what the theory says that they will. Although these tests have not been designed at this point in the process, construct validity can be applied through the process to make sure that as the tests are created that they do measure what they are designed to measure. This is another reason to look at a complete research strategy when considering or designing the research study.

Reliability, as stated above, is a measure of consistency. Tiku, Azarian, and Pecht (2007) write, “Reliability is the ability of a product or system to perform as intended” (p. 547). Unlike validity, a verification of reliability does not imply that a test is measuring what is intended. Reliability is simply a measure that a test is providing consistent results. If validity is a measure of accuracy, then reliability is a measure of precision. One challenge of scientific research is error. Establishing reliability in a test should help to reduce errors. This is because consistency should show any errors to be outside of the concentrated group. This should produce an observable measurement of errors in the statistical data.

Bias is another important factor in research. As stated above, bias consideration was a factor in selecting a random sampling method. Bias can occur when a researcher, consciously or unconsciously affects an experiment. By choosing a purposive sample, for example, bias could have entered the research by choosing survey subjects that the researcher already knew to harbor certain opinions on the subject. This is why much of the research done in the scientific community is blind to some degree. In the case of a random survey sample from an online survey tool, the researcher will not have any direct interaction with any test subject, so this will yield a blind result. This should eliminate bias from the study participant selection process. Beyond the initial sampling, there are many forms of researcher bias and areas where bias can occur. During the research phase the researcher can introduce bias by only selecting articles in the research that support one point of view. Bias can also be present when the data is analyzed and interpreted. Bias prevention or reduction is important in all scientific research. One area that can be concentrated on to reduce bias in the later stages of research is that of variable selection, or in choosing which variables to control (Soh, Harrington, & Zaslavsky, 2008).

Due to its complex nature ethics presents another challenge when executing research. Outside of research, ethics is often contrasted with legality. What is ethical is not always legal, and what is legal is not always ethical. However, this construct is very dependent on the individual's point of view or world view. The ethics of research are not as dependent on personal viewpoint, but they can still be complex, because research ethics can extend beyond the scope of a single research project. This gatekeeper role is played by many scientific institutions, whether at the university or national level. Beyond the external viewpoint, ethics, similar to bias, is important to research. One important ethical consideration is consent. In this particular research study, all survey participants must give their consent to participate in the study. This is very important for legal and ethical reasons. Beyond that it is important that the researcher follow the rules of ethics and use the data in an appropriate way. The researcher also has an ethical obligation to protect the privacy of the research participant within the study. Topic or research area does not negate the responsibility of the researcher to conduct the study in an ethical manner. In any case the researcher has an ethical responsibility to protect the identity of the participants. If comments that were made during the study were exposed, the participant could face a reprimand from their company.

Regardless of the topic being researched, ethics plays a vital role in performing a valid study.

Conclusion

Properly identifying all aspects of a quantitative research study can be challenging. All of the factors and challenges revealed by the research must be considered completely. To create an appropriate quantitative research strategy for a study on the relationship between motivation and IT project success, these challenges must be addressed directly. Determining the purpose of the research, creating a purpose statement, properly defining the target audience of the research, choosing an instrument for the collection of the data, and analyzing the resulting data must be considered. Additionally, challenges within the research itself such as validity of the information, reliability of the source, the biases possessed by the researcher and participants and the ethics all of aspects of the study must be evaluated. This research is important and valuable to the target audience, which needs to be properly defined. The completed quantitative research strategy for a study on the relationship between motivation and IT project success should allow stakeholders to make more informed and scientifically based decisions in relation to future IT projects.

Chapter 6: Vehicles for change

Introduction

Projects, especially IT projects, can be very powerful vehicles for change. They can bring change to an individual, an organization, or to an entire community. Projects can be vehicles for desired changes, or required projects can bring changes that must be adapted to. Project management can be thought of as change management from the perspective that a project is simply a series of changes that combine to make the whole. From this perspective, part of the basis of project management theories are existing change management theories. A theory of change refers to the processes by which changes come about. Within an organization, changes can be considered as organizational change. Therefore, project management at that level is organizational change management. In fact and practice it is difficult to completely separate organizational change management from project management. Andrews, Cameron, and Harris (2008) write, "The skills and knowledge which managers found most useful were those that enabled them to "make sense" of the organizational change" (p. 300). Social aspects of projects and the changes that they affect are also a part of the overall view of project management. Social factors drive projects and technology adoption, and those projects in turn affect society on some scale. The Diffusion of innovations theory is a technology acceptance theory, being first proposed by Rogers (1962), and the Diffusion of innovations theory evaluates how the deployment of new technology relates to social systems. “Diffusion is the process by which an innovation is communicated through certain channels over time among the members of a social system" (Rogers, 1962, p. 5). The social system drives the spread of the technology and the technology drives the evolution of the social system.

Managing change

What is change? Webster’s dictionary defines change as, “to make a shift from one to another.” (“Change”, 2016). Change, therefore is a shifting from one state to another and this shifting involves a process. What project managers and team members do is initiate change and manage to through this shifting process. This is why project management can be thought of as change management. Change management can include directing the processes and people that are effecting the shifting process or managing the expectations, acceptance, or understanding of the people within an organization that is changing. The project is the vehicle for change in the sense that the project contains or should contain all of the elements needed to properly complete the needed change, which may be a negative or positive change. However, being a vehicle for change also means that a project can be undertaken simply be the free will of an organization to be a purely positive endeavor that brings social benefits beyond the organization. The later idea is a more accurate way to envision the social construct of using something like a project as a vehicle for change. While change, especially social change is an integral part of modern life in a highly political and interconnected world, even change at the organizational level can have an impact on people's lives.

Managing the organization

How a project is managed and sold largely determines the perceptions of those involved or impacted by organizational change. Vakola (2014) writes, "The readiness level may vary on the basis of what employees perceive as the balance between costs and benefits of maintaining a behavior and the costs and benefits of change." (p. 195). Every person within an organization will be effected is some manner by organizational change, and will have some level of readiness to the change. Those closer to the change process or who may be impacted more by the change will likely also have a perception of the impact of the organizational change. These perception need to managed as part of the change management process as well as the actual impacts to people within the organization. Managing the attitudes, acceptance, and expectations of the stakeholders within an organization are as much a part of a project as are the functional steps that make up the project. The project team must provide support for organizational members to digest and accept change. For a project to be successful and meet all of the needs of an organization, the human elements cannot be ignored and to truly use a project as a vehicle for change a public relations element is needed. It could be considered as a wise choice to have someone from an organization's public relations department on the project team to champion the organizational change, relate it to the people, and provide counsel before and after the change. (Exploring the role of public relations in organizational change, 1994)

Managing communication

In order for a project to connect with an organization's members, they must understand the impact of the change and see the benefit to themselves and the organization. One method to control the opinions, perceptions, and acceptance of the people regarding a project is through the use of public relations and managed communication. On the success of a project phase, Uta-Micaela and Sriramesh (2004) write, "This was only possible because of the integration of the communication department right from the start of the strategy process. The management recognized that an integrated communication approach to the corporate identity process coupled with intensive public relations is a decisive factor in managing change successfully." (p. 372). Managing the relationship between the project team and the public, what is usually considered public relations, is in reality managing the communications related to the project. Managing these communications could be related to many elements of the project. One area for instance might be training. Negative perceptions about the project or change might be created when people are afraid that they will not have the knowledge to use a particular system after the changes are made. Early and informative communications about the changes to that system, details about the training that will be given, and a positive spin could eliminate these negative perceptions before they are able to for or take hold. This concept is applicable to many types of projects or scenarios. Aubert, Hooper, and Schnepel (2013) write, "Communication quality is repeatedly listed among the top success factors to consider when implementing an ERP system." (p. 64).

Managing the outcome

Whether it is described as change management or project management, the goal is the same, to manage the outcome. Regardless of the title that it is given, both of these ideas are related to managing the outcome. Managing the outcome means using all of the tools available and the elements that relate to project management to set a goal and achieve it. Setting yourself up for success in a project is like stacking the deck in your favor. This starts by understanding the change and the organization undergoing it. It includes understanding the needs of the organizations stakeholders through collecting data from them. It means finding the right people for the project team and then setting realistic goal and keeping the project of track to meet those goals. And it also means managing the scope of the project and protecting the organization from themselves and their own management in terms of unrealistic goals or timelines. Much of this falls on the shoulders of the project manager and as such the choice of project manager can make or break a project, so it is an important role. Anantatmula (2010) writes, “In spite of advances in the project management profession, research studies have shown that many projects fail, underlining the importance of the project manager's role as manager. Specifically, the manager's leadership role is of great importance in motivating people and creating an effective working environment in order for the project team to meet greater challenges in today's global economy.” (p. 13). While the specific traits of what makes a good and successful project manager might be difficult to separate as valid independent variable related to project success, the leadership role of the project manager is important to success factors related to project performance. Project success and the success of the project manager do vary, for instance you can perfectly manage a project and not meet every goal because of the technology and variations between each organization. While project success and project management success are not the same thing, success in project management or a successful project manager contributes to project success. Regardless of the elements of what makes a project successful, managing the outcome requires the full understanding and attention to all of them.

Summary

There are many factors that make a projects successful and many factors that can make a project a vehicle for change. It is the direction that the project is given, the quality of the management, and the intent of the organization that determine the value and success of each project. Change in any form can be positive or negative, it can be constructive or destructive, it can be outward facing or inward facing, and it can be reluctant or purposefully undertaken. It is when change is purposefully undertaken with the goal to have a positive and constructive outcome that the world moves forward and progress is made. Often real progress is made slowly and takes many working together to accomplish. However, when people do work together in a common goal and through teamwork, there is nothing that cannot be accomplished by the human mind, spirit, and will. Linnartz 2008 writes, “Teamwork includes cooperation, collaboration and coordination plus it greatly increases interactions of support and a sense of belonging and pride. Working as a team provides maximum opportunity for contributions to be made by individuals that benefit the team and organization. It also creates a powerful dynamic of synergy of sharing, creating and productivity.” (p. 1). Managing outcomes through teamwork is an important element in ensuring a successful project and in using a project to drive change.

Chapter 7: Leadership of Global Information Technology Projects

Introduction

The goal of this literature review is to evaluate the cultural variables critical to successful leadership of a global information technology project. Also to analyze the fundamental challenges to today's IT projects. To properly evaluate variables critical to successful leadership, a thorough investigation must be made of the leader, which in most cases will be the CIO or IT Manager. Technology acceptance is the concept of how end users accept and therefore use technology and is a key cultural variable critical to success. The concept of technology acceptance is very important and applies to a wide scope of users including both personal and business end users, IT employees and managers, and business executives. Jiun-Sheng and Hsing-Chi (2011) write, "Consumers' adoption of new information technology has been a central concern to many researchers and practitioners owing to its importance in technology diffusion." (p. 424). For the purposes of this research, the focus is on business acceptance, specifically IT managers. When presented with any new technology, many factors influence decisions made regarding the use or acceptance. This is no different than being presented anything new, whether food, tools, or toys. The human brain is very complex and any decision goes through many steps and is greatly influenced by the individual. Many of these individual influences include personal esthetic preference, culture, core values, etc. To account for these individual tastes and feeling, researchers look to behavior on a larger scale and seek to determine how technology is accepted by a larger group or population. This can be thought of as a technology acceptance model. There are many technology acceptance models that vary in how they look at human decision making. In order to select a technology acceptance model that best fits the purpose of this research several models need to be evaluated so that they can be compared and contrasted. The following models influence technology acceptance: the theory of planned behavior; the theory of reasoned action; diffusion of innovations; the technology acceptance model or TAM; the extended technology acceptance model; the unified theory of acceptance and use of technology; the task-technology fit model; the greenfield technology acceptance model; and the perceived characteristics of innovating model.

Role of the CIO

Businesses rely on IT and the CIO role far more than they used to, and that is fine as long as proper boundaries are maintained. The IT department and IT resources represent a large part of any modern business and are justified by large savings for the business in money and manpower. A few decades ago the IT department was seen as not needed at all, then as a necessary evil. Today, it is a foregone conclusion for any executive or business student that the IT department will play a large role in any company at least of medium size. So this is progress for sure, that allows the modern IT department and CIO to have a place of honor, purpose, and great responsibility. One role that is important of any CIO or IT Manager is that of leading and inspiring the IT department. Yes, the role of the CIO has expanded over the last few decades to one that provides more for the company overall, but the first duty should always be to the IT department. This may include providing leadership and direction, or maintaining a high level of moral. One way to keep moral high may be by providing newer equipment; most IT employees like to use and play with the latest toys and have good equipment for everyday use. Another way might be in providing occasional team building activities, like a weekly lunch or monthly activities that the department does together. Communications to the group and keeping everyone in the loop to company changes is also important. Treating everyone with respect and letting them know that they are doing a good job and contributing. Also, the CIO has to function as a buffer between upper management and IT department employees for many things, like programming or support issues, or corporate policies that effect the IT department. Basically, the CIO is in a position to look out, so to speak, for the people in their department, and their interests. This also includes managing the expectations of the upper management group. Another major aspect of the CIO role that has changed over time due to legal and cultural changes is the contribution to IT and corporate policies. These policies can cover a broad range of topics, from the use of thumb drives and burners to the acceptable use of corporate computers. These policies will be different in each company based on their values and circumstances. An acceptable use policy is one that is very common in most companies and may govern things like the ability to listen to music at work; this is one that might be a coordinating effort between the CIO and the HR Manager. This policy might be affected by the company's internet connection speed, which if slow might restrict the use of online music. Companies also might not want music stored on hard drives or servers for space or legal reasons. All these things and many more are factors that the modern CIO must evaluate when drafting or contributing to policies and this is an issue that can get very deep. Overall, the position of CIO is one that is far more improved and respected than it once was, to spite the complications that come with the job. I also believe that this trend will continue in the same direction in the future as the CIO role will take on more and more strategic importance in the company and corporation of tomorrow. I am currently at the IT Manager level, but once I am finished with my doctoral degree, the position of CIO is a reasonable goal for my future. I am looking forward to the challenges and opportunities that I may face if fate and determination lead me in that direction.

Cultural acceptance models

The theory of planned behavior is a theory within the field of psychology that attempts to connect a link between beliefs and behaviors, including acceptance. Although this theory helps to explain behaviors such as acceptance, it is not directly focused on technology acceptance. This theory was proposed by Icek Ajzen and based in part on the theory of reasoned action. The theory of planned behavior states that attitude toward behavior, subjective norms, and perceived behavioral control shape behavior (Ajzen, 1991). Pickett, Ginsburg, Mendez, Lim, Blankenship, Foster, and Sheffield (2012) write, "Ajzen's Theory of Planned Behavior (TPB) maintains that an individual's behavior can be predicted based on attitudes, subjective norms, perceived behavioral control, and especially, intentions." (p. 339). Within this theory, social influence is recognized as a major factor in human behavior. In the modern world of social networking and smart phones, there is a tremendous level of social pressure to conform. Therefore despite the original intentions of this theory, it has direct relevance to modern technology acceptance. The heavy use of social media and smart phones has become what Ajzen (1991) referred to as a social norm. Although this theory provides a foundation for other theories and is relevant to some types of technology acceptance, it does not directly address technology acceptance in business. While there is some level of social pressure within IT, this theory is not specific enough to this industry to be the dominating theory of the research.

Another base theory that helps to establish some of the modern technology acceptance models is the theory of reasoned action. The theory of reasoned action is a model that seeks to predict behavior and attitude. The theory of reasoned action is a theory that heavily influenced the development of the theory of planned behavior discussed above. The theory of reasoned action was also created by Icek Ajzen along with Martin Fishbein. The main components of the theory of reasoned action are: behavioral intention, attitude, and subjective norm. Attitudes is described as the sum of beliefs about a particular behavior weighted by evaluations of these beliefs. Subjective norms look at the influence of people in one's social environment on his or her behavioral intentions. Behavioral intention is a function of both attitudes toward a behavior and subjective norms toward that behavior, which has been found to predict actual behavior (Ajzen & Fishbein, 1980). Nguyen (2011) writes, "Human behavior such as cooperation can be explained by the theory of reasoned action." (p. 61). Ajzen and Fishbein make reference to subjective norm, similar to Ajzen's reference to social norm. This concept of norm, or what is normal, is a major contributing factor to the adoption or acceptance in general. This is equally relatable to technology, clothing, or behavior in general. Subjective norms continue to establish peer pressure as a potential causal factor in acceptance. Again, within the context of our modern world that has become both engrossed in and socially dependent on social media and technology, peer pressure is likely a major factor in the use of a particular technology and furthermore in the eventual or immediate acceptance of that or any technology. Like planned behavior, reasoned action helps to establish a basis for understanding behavior and acceptance, but is not focused sufficiently on technology. Therefore it is not relevant enough to the IT industry to use as the basis for technology acceptance research.

Diffusion of innovations is one of the first major technology acceptance theories or models, being first proposed by Rogers (1962). Diffusion of innovations evaluates new technology and how it is spread though a culture. “Diffusion is the process by which an innovation is communicated through certain channels over time among the members of a social system" (Rogers, 1962, p. 5). These certain channels in the modern world include the various protocols that make use of the internet. The speed of communication in modern social systems like social media extends and magnifies the significance of this theory. This theory relies heavily on human interaction and supposes that a technology must be widely adopted before it reaches a self-sustaining level. The diffusion of innovations theory suggests that four main factors effect acceptance: the innovation or actual technology, available communication channels, time, and the existence of a social system. The diffusion of innovations theory also provides four basic categories of technology adopters: innovators, early adopters, early majority, and late majority. Additionally the diffusion of innovations theory lists five stages of the technology acceptance process: knowledge, persuasion, decision, implementation, and confirmation (Rogers, 1962). A question remains as to whether or not this social aspect that permeates the acceptance theories explored thus far extends to business environments, specifically in the IT industry. Despite the age of the theory, diffusion of innovation is still relevant theory utilized in our modern society. Kilmon and Fagan (2007) write, “A case study approach was taken using a component of diffusion of innovations theory as a framework for exploring the research questions." (p. 134). This suggests that the diffusion of innovations theory has potential as the technology acceptance model that would serve as a basis for the research framework for an IT industry related study. This theory is very robust in the description of the various elements of technology adoption and stands as a strong candidate for research on the IT industry.

One technology acceptance theory, simply called the technology acceptance model or TAM, models technology use and acceptance. The technology acceptance model identifies factors that influence decisions related to acceptance and use of technology. Two prominent factors noted are perceived usefulness and perceived ease of use (Davis, 1989). Davis (1989) defines perceived usefulness as "the degree to which a person believes that using a particular system would enhance his or her job performance." (p. 319). Davis (1989) defines perceived ease of use as "the degree to which a person believes that using a particular system would be free from effort." (p. 319). The technology acceptance model is based on the theory of reasoned action, explored above. The technology acceptance model also identifies constraints, such as the limited freedom to act. Ease of use is an important concept introduced by the technology acceptance model and may be an important part of applying a technology acceptance model to the IT industry. Ease of use is important because many users have difficulty in learning to use new technology even when the features are very similar in use to the old technology that they are more comfortable with. The technology acceptance model is in very wide use and is very adaptable. Pasaoglu (2011) writes, "The technology acceptance model (TAM) is another theoretical model commonly used for predicting and explaining user behavior and IT usage." (p. 157). The technology acceptance model was one of the few early theories that looked at human behavior within the context of the technology explosion of the late 1970's and early 1980's. This is the same technology boom that gave rise to companies like Apple and Microsoft. This is a core technology acceptance model that many newer models are built on or adapted from. The technology acceptance model is still popular for direct adaptation and use in modern technology acceptance research. As such, this theory has high potential for use with research with the IT industry.

The unified theory of acceptance and use of technology is a technology acceptance model that seeks to explain a user's intentions and behavior. This theory was formulated by Venkatesh, Morris, Davis, and Davis (2003). The theory has four key elements: performance expectancy, effort expectancy, social influence, and facilitating conditions. The Unified theory of acceptance and use of technology also lists four variables that Venkatesh, Morris, Davis, and Davis (2003) call "direct determinant of use behavior." (p. 425). These determinants are: gender, age, experience, and voluntariness of use (Venkatesh, Morris, Davis, & Davis, 2003). This is the first theory that mentions age and gender. Variables like age and gender allow for correlation in the research analysis and produce stronger research results. The unified theory of acceptance and use of technology is based on several other theories, including: the theory of reasoned action, the theory of planned behavior, diffusion of innovations theory, and the technology acceptance model. This is a good example of how research extends the stream of knowledge and how each new theory build on those proposed before it. Venkatesh, Morris, Davis, and Davis (2003) write, "Information technology acceptance research has yielded many competing models, each with different sets of acceptance determinants." (p. 425). There are many different theories related to the acceptance of technology, many of which explore the same or similar themes like social pressure and communication. The only drawback to this theory is that while is seeks to unify multiple theories, it relies on over forty variables, which will likely exceed the scope of a research study on the IT industry. The unified theory of acceptance and use of technology model would likely require much more time and detailed data than a simpler model like the diffusion of innovation model.

The extended technology acceptance model is based on the TAM, or technology acceptance model. It is sometimes referred to as TAM2. The extended technology acceptance model was developed by Venkatesh and Davis, who were principle contributors to the unified theory of acceptance and use of technology theory. The extended technology acceptance model is a theoretical extension of the TAM, or technology acceptance model that evaluated usefulness and usage intentions in terms of social influence (Venkatesh & Davis, 2000). On this point, Venkatesh and Davis write:

> The extended model was strongly supported for all four organizations at all three points of measurement, accounting for 40%-60% of the variance in usefulness perceptions and 34%-52% of the variance in usage intentions. Both social influence processes (subjective norm, voluntariness, and image) and cognitive instrumental processes (job relevance, output quality, result demonstrability, and perceived ease of use) significantly influenced user acceptance. (Venkatesh & Davis, 2000, p. 186)

The findings within their research suggest that this combination of factors, when combined, greatly expands the understanding of technology adoption behavior (Venkatesh & Davis, 2000). The extended technology acceptance model is a significant improvement over the technology acceptance model, without the complexity of the unified theory of acceptance and use of technology. The extended technology acceptance model has great potential to be used as the primary model for the research on IT project success.

Most of the theories or models discussed to this point have been very general in their target population, specifically normal technology user rather business or IT industry users. The Greenfeld technology acceptance model is specifically designed to evaluate technology acceptance within nonprofit organizations. It is important to evaluate the Greenfeld technology acceptance model for potential research use or adaptation for the general IT industry. This is because it is necessary to understanding the ability to adapt models. Greenfeld and Rohde (2011) write, “During the past decade there has been an increasing interest in research within Not-for-Profit (NFP) organizations. Research has indicated that there are a number of characteristics that make NFPs different from other organizations.” (p. 26). The Greenfeld technology acceptance model was developed by Greenfeld and Rohde and based on the technology acceptance model or TAM. The Greenfeld technology acceptance model was developed because there was a concern that the technology acceptance model or TAM was not able to predict across all situations (Greenfeld & Rohde, 2011). This is a concern, as many of the contemporary technology acceptance models are based, at least in part, on the technology acceptance model. The Greenfeld technology acceptance model suggests that career choice is a variable the technology acceptance model does not account for. The career choice of an individual likely reveals something deeper about their psychology and may be a significant factor in their behavior, attitude, perceived usefulness, and perceived ease of use in relation to technology that effect their individual technology acceptance (Greenfeld & Rohde, 2011). This suggests that that this model might be used if the research study on the IT industry were limited to IT departments within the nonprofit sector. This may also suggest that a new and independent model is needed, possibly to be developed as part of this independent IT industry research project.

The task-technology fit model is a very simple model that is specific to the IT industry that does not directly address acceptance, but instead addresses utilization, as well as individual performance. This theory was developed by Goodhue and Thompson in 1995. Goodhue and Thompson identified four total variables: task characteristics, technology characteristics, performance impacts, and utilization. Additionally the task-technology fit theory proposes that there is a direct relationship between task characteristics and technology characteristics to performance impacts and utilization. Most importantly, the theory makes the argument that information system or technology and the intended technology benefits are achieved when the technology is well suited for the task. This is a simple concept, but likely a significant factor of variable in overall technology acceptance (Goodhue & Thompson, 1995). Goodhue and Thompson (1995) define task-technology fit (TTF) as "the extent to which a technology provides features and supports a fit with the requirements of the task." (p. 213). Describing the application of the task-technology fit theory, Forman (2014) writes, "From an organizational perspective, the more an organization perceives a technological fit, the more likely that technology will be utilized" (p.41). This is shows that the task-technology fit theory, despite being simple in design, exposes the same reliance on social systems and communication for the acceptance of technology that is detailed in many other technology acceptance models. However the task-technology fit theory is more compact in design and potentially more efficient as a model when inserted as part of a complete research strategy. Many research studies that employed the task-technology fit model as a core part of research strategy were discovered during the research. This suggests the theory is well suited to be adapted to many specific technologies within the IT industry. This is likely due to the simplicity and flexibility. However, a model with very few variables may not provide enough of a theoretical construct to meet the needs of research specific to the IT industry.

The perceived characteristics of innovating model, or PCI, developed by Moore and Benbaset in 1991 identifies elements that are fundamental to technology adoption. The perceived characteristics of innovating model identifies four factors that influence the adoption of innovation or technology: image, result demonstrability, visibility, and voluntariness (Moore & Benbasat, 1991). These factors vary from the previous models explored, but they are valid none the less. Image, one of the identified factors, is a used to market technology today and it has a large effect of sales. A simple look at the marketing surrounding the many Apple products on the market make the power of image very evident. This also connects the concept of image to that of the social construct that many other technology acceptance models have focused on. The image that a technology has or presents is largely driven by social factors. Additionally, the perceived characteristics of innovating identifies two additional constructs: relative advantage and compatibility. There are potential problem with the model. The perceived characteristics of innovating model is industry specific as originally envisioned, similar to the Greenfeld technology acceptance model. In the case of the perceived characteristics of innovating model, it was developed to evaluate the adoption of innovation within government. Additionally, like the Greenfeld technology acceptance model, the perceived characteristics of innovating model could be used for IT industry research that was limited to a specific job sector. So, one potential option would be to use the model for a research study within government IT departments. However, the model could also be modified or adapted to apply to the whole IT industry or just private sector IT departments.

To this point, the research has encompassed several technology acceptance models or theories. Many have common themes, such as social pressure and communications. Outside of these structured technology acceptance models, one question remains as a gap in this research thus far. That question is, beyond the obvious factors that affect technology acceptance, what underlying or subconscious drivers are responsible. In researching an answer to this question, Maslow's hierarchy of needs was coming up often in the research. Maslow's hierarchy of needs, is a theory by Abraham Maslow introduced in 1943 in a paper called a theory of human motivation. In the theory of human motivation, Maslow (1943), describes his observations of the innate nature of humans. In the theory of human motivation, Maslow (1943), developed a hierarchy of needs that included the following, in order of the most basic to the most evolved: physiological, safety, belongingness or love, esteem, and self-actualization (Maslow, 1943). It is the needs of belongingness and esteem that best relate to the social aspect of technology acceptance. On this relationship, Cao, Jiang, Oh, Li, Liao, & Chen (2013) write, "In level three, we find needs of belonging and love that are also termed social needs, including love, be loved, and a sense of belonging." (p. 170). According to Maslow (1943), humans need a sense of belonging and acceptance as humans, and this comes from our social groups, whether large or small. (Maslow, 1943) This theory seems to be connected to acceptance to a degree that on that strength alone it should have a connection to this research on technology acceptance in the IT industry. Outside of the ability to feel socially connected and accepted by using certain technology, some technological device can also serve as a surrogate for human social networks. An additional aspect of technology acceptance in modern times may be the extent to which a technology serves as a social surrogate. Esteem is also a factor, as much of our modern identity is tied to what technology humans are able to possess. Technology can be a status symbol. Today, people usually carry their smart phone in such a way that the screen size is obvious to any observer, and this is part of that is part of modern identity within the western culture. This is true as well within the IT industry and Business in general. Businesses tend to provide technology as a benefit to certain positions within a company, and that can be a badge of rank. The simple providing of a laptop or cell phone as part of your benefit package within a company can elevate social status within the company.

Conclusion

Several different theories related to the acceptance of technology have been explored. Seminal articles were a core part of this effort. Some of which could be forcibly applied to the specific field or industry of Information Technology. Others, however, where specifically designed and conceived for this application. Some were very specific in scope or industry, and others very vague. One very common theme revealed was the social aspect of technology acceptance and how peer-pressure and social acceptance drive technology acceptance. This research, while focused on business acceptance within the IT industry cannot ignore this strong relationship between technology acceptance and social systems. The diffusion of innovations theory, though not a new model, seems to be very relevant to the overall process of technology acceptance within the context of social media. Lane and Coleman (2012) write:

> "The advance of the use of social networking systems is rapid and compelling. People are continually connected to each other on their blackberries, i-phones, netbooks and computers. People are texting, talking, e-mailing and in general, communicating through electronic rather than face-to-face methods at an accelerating pace." (Lane & Coleman, 2012, p. 1)

Social media accelerates or magnifies several of the factors identified by the diffusion of innovations model: communication channels, time, and a social system (Rogers, 1962). The model that best suits this research may be a modified diffusion of innovations model that directly accounts for social networking. Social networking is a technology that magnifies the effects of behavioral influences. Because many behavioral influences are present in a real time environment, the social network acts like a catalyst to the behavioral reaction. This is similar to the process of heat catalyzing a chemical reaction. Within the ecosystem of a social network time, communication, and social interaction frequency are increased well beyond what is normal or common. Social networking is relevant to the IT industry as it is to other industries. Many companies now have a social networking presence and monitor the lives and actions of employees. This relationship is relevant to the study of behavior and to the workers within the IT industry. Knowing how social networking affects technology acceptance in the workplace needs to understood as part of any research effort.

REFERENCES

Adams, J. S. (1965). Inequity in social exchange. Advances in experimental social psychology, 276-299.

Ajzen, I. & Fishbein, M. (1980). Understanding attitudes and predicting social behavior. Englewood Cliffs, NJ: Prentice-Hall.

Ajzen, I. (1991). The theory of planned behavior. *Organizational Behavior and Human Decision Processes 50* (2), 179–211.

Ameen, R. Y., & Hamo, A. Y. (2013). Survey of server virtualization. *International Journal of Computer Science and Information Security, 11*(3), 65-74. Retrieved from http://search.proquest.com/docview /1467463127

Anantatmula, V. S. (2010). Project manager leadership role in improving Project performance. *Engineering Management Journal, 22*(1), 13-22. Retrieved from http://search.proquest.com/docview/734620101

Andrews, J., Cameron, H., & Harris, M. (2008). All change? managers' experience of organizational change in theory and practice. *Journal of Organizational Change Management, 21*(3), 300-314. doi:http://dx.doi.org/10.1108/09534810810874796

Andrew, G. M., Theresa, M. G., & Hulin, C. (2005). Experience sampling mood and its correlates at work. Journal of Occupational and Organizational Psychology, 78, 171-193. Retrieved from http://search.proquest.com/docview/199349185

Ann, C. L. (1998). Bridging positivist and interpretivist approaches to qualitative methods. *Policy Studies Journal, 26*(1), 162-180. Retrieved from http://search.proquest.com/docview/210560612

Aubert, B., Hooper, V., & Schnepel, A. (2013). Revisiting the role of communication quality in ERP project success. *American Journal of Business, 28*(1), 64-85. doi:http://dx.doi.org/10.1108/19355181311314770

Bele, R., & Desai, C. (2012). Review on virtualization: In the light of storage and server virtualization technology. Journal of Information and Operations Management, 3(1), 245-249. Retrieved from http://search.proquest.com/docview/1019052148

Bhunia, A. (2013). Statistical methods for practice and research (A guide to data analysis using SPSS). *South Asian Journal of Management, 20*(1), 154-157. Retrieved from http://search.proquest.com/docview/1370705490

Bizarro, P. A., & Garcia, A. (2013). VIRTUALIZATION: BENEFITS, RISKS, AND CONTROL. *Internal Auditing, 28*(4), 11-18. Retrieved from http://search.proquest.com/docview/143199165

Bologa, A., & Bologa, R. (2011). A perspective on the benefits of data virtualization technology. *Informatica Economica, 15*(4), 110-118. Retrieved from http://search.proquest.com/docview/922387768

Bridges, D. (2013). STREAMLINING OPERATIONS THROUGH VIRTUALIZATION. *Bank News, 113*(8), 14-15. Retrieved from http://search.proquest.com/docview/1428959788

Brown, K. A., & Ki, E. (2013). Developing a valid and reliable measure of organizational crisis responsibility. *Journalism and Mass Communication Quarterly, 90*(2), 363-384. Retrieved from http://search.proquest.com/docview/1445173142

Cao, H., Jiang, J., Oh, L., Li, H., Liao, X., & Chen, Z. (2013). A maslow's hierarchy of needs analysis of social networking services continuance. *Journal of Service Management, 24*(2), 170-190. doi:http://dx.doi.org/10.1108/09564231311323953

Carmeli, A., Elizur, D., & Yaniv, E. (2007). The theory of work commitment: A facet analysis. *Personnel Review, 36*(4), 638-649. doi:http://dx.doi.org/10.1108/00483480710752849

Change [Def. 2]. (n.d.). *Merriam-Webster Online.* In Merriam-Webster. Retrieved June 8, 2016, from http://www.merriam-webster.com/dictionary/change.

Chun, M., & Mooney, J. (2009). CIO roles and responsibilities: Twenty-five years of evolution and change, Information and Management, v.46 n.6,p.323-334.

Connor, D. (2004). Server virtualization is on the rise. Network World, 21(49), 25-25, 28. Retrieved from http://search.proquest.com/docview/215981425

Davis, F. D. (1989). Perceived usefulness, perceived ease of use, and user acceptance of information technology, *MIS Quarterly, 13*(3), 319–340.

Day, E. (1997). Qualitative research course emphasizes understanding merits and limitations. Marketing News, 31(16), 9-9. Retrieved from http://search.proquest.com/docview/216406710

Danko, M. P. (2010). A phenomenological study of time managment. (Order No. 3414557, University of Phoenix). ProQuest Dissertations and Theses, , 162-n/a. Retrieved from http://search.proquest.com/docview/733882445

Dicicco-Bloom, B., & Crabtree, B. F. (2006). The qualitative research interview. Retrieved from http://www.ncbi.nlm.nih.gov/pubmed/16573666

Dube, L., Bernier, C., & Roy, V. (2009). Taking on the Challenge of IT Management in a Global Business Context: The Alcan Case (Part A and B). International Journal of Case Studies in Management, 7(2).

Dubie, D. (2009). Weighing desktop virtualization. Network World, 26(22), 16-16, 32. Retrieved from http://search.proquest.com/docview/215993472

Elizabeth, W. B., Al-Gahtani, S., & Hubona, G. S. (2007). The effects of gender and age on new technology implementation in a developing country. *Information Technology & People, 20*(4), 352-375. doi:http://dx.doi.org/10.1108/09593840710839798

Exploring the role of public relations in organizational change. 1994). *The Public Relations Journal, 50*(8), 52. Retrieved from http://search.proquest.com/docview/195921162

Forman, H. (2014). BUYING CENTERS AND THE ROLE OF SUPPLY CHAIN ORIENTATION ON NEW INFORMATION TECHNOLOGY SATISFACTION IN THE AUTOMOTIVE INDUSTRY. *Journal of Marketing Theory and Practice, 22*(1), 41-52. Retrieved from http://search.proquest.com/docview/1477880652

Frels, R. K., & Onwuegbuzie, A. J. (2013). Administering quantitative instruments with qualitative interviews: A mixed research approach. Journal of Counseling and Development : JCD, 91(2), 184-194. Retrieved from http://search.proquest.com/docview/1330852078

Gareiss, R. (2008). Desktop virtualization helps deliver functionality to virtual workers.*Network World (Online),* Retrieved from http://search.proquest.com/docview /223737798

Goodhue, D. L., & Thompson, R. L. (1995) Task-technology fit and individual performance, *MIS Quarterly, 1995, 19*, 2, 213-236.

Greenfeld, G., & Rohde, F. H. (2011). Technology acceptance: Are NFPs or their workers different?. *International Journal of Information Systems and Social Change, 2 2*, 26-36.

Grisham, T. (2009). The delphi technique: A method for testing complex and multifaceted topics. International Journal of Managing Projects in Business, 2(1), 112-130. doi:http://dx.doi.org/10.1108/17538370910930545

Hackman, J. R., & Oldham, G. R. (1976). Motivation through the design of work: Test of a theory. Organizational Behavior and Human Performance, 16, 250-279.

Hamersly, B., & Land, D. (2015). Building productivity in virtual project teams. *Revista De Gestão e Projetos, 6*(1), 1. Retrieved from https://search.proquest.com/docview/1696144683

Hassell, J. (2007). Server virtualization: GETTING STARTED. Computerworld, 41(22), 31-31. Retrieved from http://search.proquest.com/docview/216090475

Herzberg, F. (1964). The Motivation-Hygiene Concept and Problems of Manpower. *Personnel Administrator*, (27), 3–7.

Higgins, E. T. (1987). Self-discrepancy: A theory relating self and affect. *Psychological Review,94*, 319-340

Hookway, B. (2010). Low cost Android: crossing the $100 barrier. on VisionMobile Blog. Retrieved from https://www.visionmobile.com/blog/2010/02/low-cost-android-crossing-the-100-barrier

HP. (2009). "Server virtualization technologies for x86-based HP Blade System and HP ProLiant servers technology brief, 3rd edition". Hewlett-Packard Development Company, L.P.

Hsieh, C. (2008). Strategies for successfully implementing a virtualization project: A case with VMware. Communications of the IIMA, 8(3), 1-I. Retrieved from http://search.proquest.com/docview/ 205911370

Hull, C. L. (1935). The Conflicting Psychologies of Learning: A Way Out. Psychological Review, 42, 491-516.

Hung, P., & Low, G. C. (2008). Factors affecting the buy vs build decision in large australian organisations. Journal of Information Technology, 23(2), 118-131. doi:http://dx.doi.org/10.1057/palgrave.jit.2000098

Husky, M. M., Mazure, C. M., Carroll, K. M., Barry, D., & Petry, N. M. (2008). Using the experience sampling method in the context of contingency management for substance abuse treatment. Journal of Applied Behavior Analysis, 41(4), 635-44. Retrieved from http://search.proquest.com/docview/225031392

ISO 9000. (n.d.). In Wikipedia. Retrieved February 15, 2013, from http://en.wikipedia.org/wiki/ISO_9001.

ISO 9001 proven to help win new business. (2001). Retrieved from http://www.british-assessment.co.uk/news/iso-9001-proven-to-help-win-new-business.

Jiun-Sheng, C. L., & Hsing-Chi, C. (2011). The role of technology readiness in self-service technology acceptance. *Managing Service Quality, 21*(4), 424-444. doi:http://dx.doi.org/10.1108/09604521111146289

Kennedy, R. C. (2007). Application and desktop virtualization. InfoWorld, 29(7), 28-28,30,32. Retrieved from http://search.proquest.com/ docview/194365643

Kevork, E. K., & Vrechopoulos, A. P. (2009). CRM literature: Conceptual and functional insights by keyword analysis. Marketing Intelligence & Planning, 27(1), 48-85. doi:http://dx.doi.org/10.1108/02634500910928362

Khalifa, M. H. E. (2011). Perceptions of equity and job satisfaction: A study of university employees in egypt. *International Journal of Management, 28*(4), 130-143,195. Retrieved from http://search.proquest.com/docview/902631516

Kharuddin, S., Ashhari, Z. M., & Nassir, A. M. (2010). Information system and firms' performance: The case of Malaysian small medium enterprises. *International Business Research, 3*(4), 28-35. Retrieved from http://search.proquest.com/docview/822629352

Kilmon, C., & Fagan, M. H. (2007). Course management software adoption: A diffusion of innovations perspective. *Campus - Wide Information Systems, 24*(2), 134-144. doi:http://dx.doi.org/10.1108/10650740710742736

Kontzer, T. (2010). Virtualization as a tool for agile it. CIO Insight, (113), 28-31. Retrieved from http://search.proquest.com/docview/755009140

Kovar, J. F. (2008). Virtualization's dream team -- our exclusive research reveals just how hot virtualization is. no need to tell the folks at VMware. CRN, (1257), 22-24. Retrieved from http://search.proquest.com/docview/227559156

Kunz, J., & Quitmann, A. (2011). Der einfluss von anreizsystemen auf die Intrinsische Motivation/The influence of incentive systems on intrinsic motivation. *Zeitschrift Für Personalforschung, 25*(1), 55-76. Retrieved from http://search.proquest.com/docview/849287739

Lane, M., & Coleman, P. (2012). Technology ease of use through social networking media. *Journal of Technology Research, 3*, 1-12. Retrieved from http://search.proquest.com/docview/1022984844

Lehning, J. (2013). Community college presidents in a southern state: An exploratory qualitative inquiry of servant leadership. (Order No. 3561673, Capella University). ProQuest Dissertations and Theses, , 167. Retrieved from http://search.proquest.com/docview/1364620454

Linnartz, B. (2008, Mar 06). MANAGEMENT CORNER: TOOLS FOR WORKING AS A TEAM. *The Taos News* Retrieved from http://search.proquest.com/docview/251673651

Locke, E. A. (1976). The nature and causes of job satisfaction. Handbook of industrial and organizational psychology: 1297-1350.

Mansourian, Y. (2008). Exploratory nature of, and uncertainty tolerance in, qualitative research. *New Library World, 109*(5), 273-286. doi:http://dx.doi.org/10.1108/03074800810873614

Maslow, A. H. (1943). A theory of human motivation. Psychological Review, 50(4), 370–96.

McAllister, N. (2007). Server virtualization. InfoWorld, 29(7), 20-22. Retrieved from http://search.proquest.com/docview/194379931

Melucci, N. (2010). E-Z Psychology. New York: Barron's Educational Series, Inc.

Michailidis, M. P., & Dracou, N. (2011). The job redesigning process: A study of medical representatives using the job characteristics model. *The Business Review, Cambridge, 17*(1), 228-234. Retrieved from http://search.proquest.com/docview/871194106

Moore, G. C., & Benbasat, I. (1991). Development of an instrument to measure the perceptions of adopting an information technology innovation, *Information Systems Research, 2*(3), 173-191.

Moustakas, C. (1994). Phenomenological Research Methods. Thousand Oaks, CA: Sage Publications, Inc.

Myers, D. G. (2011). Exploring psychology, eighth edition. New York: Worth Publishers.

Nguyen, N. P. (2011). Applying "theory of reasoned action" to explain inter-firm cooperation: Empirical evidence from Vietnamese enterprises. *International Journal of Management and Information Systems, 15*(3), 61-81. Retrieved from http://search.proquest.com/docview/880246708

Norall, S. (2007). Storage virtualization. InfoWorld, 29(7), 24-27. Retrieved from http://search. proquest.com/docview/194380632

Palethorpe, R., & Wilson, J. P. (2011). Learning in the panic zone: Strategies for managing learner anxiety. *Journal of European Industrial Training, 35*(5), 420-438. doi:http://dx.doi.org/10.1108/03090591111138008

Pasaoglu, D. (2011). Analysis of ERP usage with technology acceptance model. *Global Business and Management Research, 3*(2), 157-165. Retrieved from http://search.proquest.com/docview/900315425

Peggy, B. K. (2007). Virtualization reality by optimizing computing resources, virtualization can lower infrastructure operating costs while improving business agility and speed to market. Insurance & Technology, 32(8), 42-42. Retrieved from http://search.proquest.com/docview/229242758

Pickett, L. L., Ginsburg, H. J., Mendez, R. V., Lim, D. E., Blankenship, K. R., Foster, L. E., . . . Sheffield, S. B. (2012). Ajzen's theory of planned behavior as it relates to eating disorders and body satisfaction. *North American Journal of Psychology, 14*(2), 339-354. Retrieved from http://search.proquest.com /docview/1013609958

Pogarcic, I., Krnjak, D., & Ozanic, D. (2012). Business benefits from the virtualization of an ICT infrastructure. *International Journal of Engineering Business Management, 4* Retrieved from http://search.proquest.com/docview/1524214856

Rabhi, F. A., Yao, L., & Guabtni, A. (2012). ADAGE: A framework for supporting user-driven ad-hoc data analysis processes. *Computing.Archives for Informatics and Numerical Computation, 94*(6), 489-519. doi:http://dx.doi.org/10.1007/s00607-012-0193-0

Ram, P. (2013). Relationship between job satisfaction and job performance in the public sector-A case study from india. *International Journal of Academic Research in Economics and Management Sciences, 2*(2), 16-35. Retrieved from http://search.proquest.com/docview/1439969241

Reichhardt, T. (1999). A million volunteers join the online search for extraterrestrial life. *Nature, 400*(6747), 804. doi:http://dx.doi.org/10.1038/23549

Rogers, E. M. (1962). Diffusion of Innovations. Glencoe, IL: Free Press.

Rouse, M., & Madden, J. (2013). Desktop Virtualization. In Techtarget. Retrieved from http://searchvirtualdesktop.techtarget.com/definition/desktop-virtualization

Sandford, L. L. (2006). Increase ISO 9001's value. Quality Progress, 39(8), 84-85. Retrieved from http://search.proquest.com/docview/214767155

Siddiqui, A., & Saba, I. (2013). Determining the job satisfaction level of the academic staff at tertiary academic institutes of pakistan. *International Journal of Information, Business and Management, 5*(3), 42-53. Retrieved from http://search.proquest.com/docview/1511381953

Schultz, B. (2009). The changing face of virtualization. Network World, 26(26), 28-30. Retrieved from http://search.proquest.com/docview/215993000

Skinner, B. F. (1978). The experimental analysis of behavior (a history). In B. F. Skinner, Reflections on behaviorism and society (pp. 113-126). Englewood Cliffs, NJ: Prentice Hall.

Sneed, B. C. A. (2006). A phenomenological study of involuntary terminations of chief executive officers. (Order No. 3220546, University of Phoenix). ProQuest Dissertations and Theses, , 154-154 p. Retrieved from http://search.proquest.com/docview/304913764

Soh, C., Harrington, D. P., & Zaslavsky, A. M. (2008). Reducing bias in parameter estimates from stepwise regression in proportional hazards regression with right-censored data. *Lifetime Data Analysis, 14*(1), 65-85. doi:http://dx.doi.org/10.1007/s10985-007-9078-5

Spiegel, E. (2006). Real world virtualization: Realizing the business benefits of application and server virtualization. Computer Technology Review, 26(2), 8-8, 26. Retrieved from http://search.proquest.com/docview/220622762

Sproull, L., & Kiesler, S. (1986). REDUCING SOCIAL CONTEXT CUES: ELECTRONIC MAIL IN ORGANIZATIONAL COMMUNICATION. *Management Science (1986-1998), 32*(11), 1492. Retrieved from http://search.proquest.com/docview/205876410

Staw, B. M., Bell, N. E., & Clausen, J. A. (1986). The dispositional approach to job attitudes: A lifetime longitudinal test. *Administrative Science Quarterly, 31*(1), 56-77.

Teeter, J. (2011). Flexible medical-grade networks. *IT Professional Magazine, 13*(3), 48-51. doi:http://dx.doi.org/10.1109/MITP.2010.119

Tiku, S., Azarian, M., & Pecht, M. (2007). Using a reliability capability maturity model to benchmark electronics companies. *The International Journal of Quality & Reliability Management, 24*(5), 547-563. doi:http://dx.doi.org/10.1108/02656710710748394

Tillman, C. J., Smith, F. A., & Tillman, W. R. (2010). WORK LOCUS OF CONTROL AND THE MULTI-DIMENSIONALITY OF JOB SATISFACTION. *Journal of Organizational Culture, Communication and Conflict, 14*(2), 107-125. Retrieved from http://search.proquest.com/docview/763234809

Uta-Micaela, D., & Sriramesh, K. (2004). Public relations and change management: The case of a multinational company. *Journal of Communication Management,8*(4), 372-383. Retrieved from http://search.proquest.com/docview/232917086

Vakola, M. (2014). What's in there for me? individual readiness to change and the perceived impact of organizational change. *Leadership & Organization Development Journal, 35*(3), 195-209. doi:http://dx.doi.org/10.1108/LODJ-05-2012-0064

Venkatesh, V., & Davis, F. D. (2000). A theoretical extension of the technology acceptance model: Four longitudinal field studies. *Management Science, 46*(2), 186–204

Venkatesh, V., Morris, M. G., Davis, G. B., & Davis, F. D. (2003). User acceptance of information technology: Toward a unified view1. *MIS Quarterly, 27*(3), 425-478. Retrieved from http://search.proquest.com/docview/218137148

Violino, B. (2009). Virtualization's new frontier. *CIO Insight,* (101), 28-30,32-33. Retrieved http://search.proquest.com/docview/213016211

Virtualize Your IT Infrastructure. (2012). Retrieved October 15, 2012, from http://www.vmware.com/virtualization/

Von Hagen, W. (2008). *Professional Xen Virtualization.* Hoboken, NJ:Wiley Publishing, Inc.

Weil, N. (2007). Storage virtualization takes off ; virtualization can help you radically speed up
backup and disaster recovery, while trimming costs. but do not bring your old ideas about management to this party. check out our advice from the trenches on how to get the best results. *CIO, 20*(23), 1. Retrieved from http://search.proquest.com/docview/205950265

Weill, P., Ross, J. W. (2008). Mechanisms for Implementing IT Governance, retrieved from http://cb.hbsp.harvard.edu/cb/pl/12928025/129280 49/50606ef0d19c2a7eebd297a947c12e6f.

Weill, P., Ross, J. W. (2009). Allocating Decision Rights and Accountability: Elements of Effective IT Governance, retrieved from http://hbr.org/product /allocating-decision-rights-accountability-elements/ an/3595BC-PDF-ENG.

Wester, K. L., Borders, L. D., Boul, S., & Horton, E. (2013). Research quality: Critique of quantitative articles in the journal of counseling & development. *Journal of Counseling and Development : JCD, 91*(3), 280-290. Retrieved from http://search.proquest.com/docview/1398803509

Yerkes, R. and Dodson, J. (1908). The relation of strength of stimulus to rapidity of habit-formation, Journal of Comparative Neurology and Psychology, Vol. 18, p. 459.

Yoshida, H. (2008). Reinventing storage virtualization. Network World, 25(39), 25-25. Retrieved from http://search.proquest.com/docview/215994613

Zhai, Q., Lindorff, M., & Cooper, B. (2013). Workplace guanxi: Its dispositional antecedents and mediating role in the affectivity-job satisfaction relationship. *Journal of Business Ethics, 117*(3), 541-551. doi:http://dx.doi.org/10.1007/s10551-012-1544-7

www.ingramcontent.com/pod-product-compliance
Lightning Source LLC
Chambersburg PA
CBHW071203050326
40689CB00011B/2228
* 9 7 8 1 5 1 1 9 6 3 9 6 1 *